Reclaiming Christianity

A.W. Tozer

Compiled and Edited by James L. Snyder

Reclaiming Christianity

A Call to Authentic Faith

Regal

From Gospel Light
Ventura, California, U.S.A.

Published by Regal
From Gospel Light
Ventura, California, U.S.A.
www.regalbooks.com
Printed in the U.S.A.

Library of Congress Cataloging-in-Publication Data
Tozer, A. W. (Aiden Wilson), 1897-1963.
Reclaiming Christianity : a call to authentic faith/ A. W. Tozer ;
compiled and edited by James L. Snyder.
p. cm.
ISBN 978-0-8307-4690-3 (trade paper)
1. Christianity. 2. Church. I. Snyder, James L. II. Title.
BR123.T66 2009
230—dc22
2009004474

1 2 3 4 5 6 7 8 9 10 / 15 14 13 12 11 10 09

Rights for publishing this book outside the U.S.A. or in
non-English languages are administered by Gospel Light Worldwide,
an international not-for-profit ministry. For additional information,
please visit www.glww.org, email info@glww.org, or write to
Gospel Light Worldwide, 1957 Eastman Avenue,
Ventura, CA 93003, U.S.A.

CONTENTS

A Prophet Looks at the Church

The Church of Jesus Christ has had no greater lover or fiercer critic than Aiden Wilson Tozer (1897-1963). During his lifetime, many regarded him as a prophet and listened to what he said or read what he wrote with a certain degree of anticipation. Some did not agree with him on everything, but they recognized that his voice was an authentic one, and that somewhere in his voice was the voice of God. When Tozer spoke, they knew that they would hear from someone who had heard from God. The hallmark of his ministry was his emphasis on what he felt was the decline of Christianity.

The Decline of Christianity

The heartbeat of Dr. Tozer's ministry was to call the Church back to her roots. It was his belief that the Christian Church was losing ground in the world and that somebody needed to call people to return to authentic faith in Jesus Christ. Comparing contemporary Christianity with the Christianity of the Bible, he saw a clear departure from the authentic spirituality seen in Scripture.

Tozer's criticism of the Church flowed from a heart that above all else loved the Head of the Church—Jesus Christ. You cannot listen to Tozer's words or read any of his books without being impressed by his intense love and appreciation for the second person of the Trinity. Anything that in any way challenged the person or authority of Christ brought him to his feet. He measured everything in the Church by this one criterion: Does it exalt Jesus Christ?

As well, you cannot help but notice in Dr. Tozer's sermons and writing that he had a tremendous love for the Body of Christ. He loved Christians of all shades and degrees of intensity. He loved Christians who were well read in theology as well as those who were simple believers in what they called "The Book." He even admired those Christians he disagreed with on a number of issues. He never made doctrine a litmus test for fellowship but enjoyed a wide variety of fellowship among many denominations. In the course of a week, he might preach in a Lutheran church, a Baptist church, a Presbyterian church, a Mennonite church or even a Pentecostal church. The name on the building did not mean very much to him as long as he found in it people that he called "The Fellowship of the Burning Heart." And out of that great love for the Church came his criticism of it.

One time, he was scheduled to preach at what was termed a "holiness church." It was some sort of a celebration or anniversary for the church, and prior to Dr. Tozer preaching, they had all kinds of frivolous activities, such as cutting each other's ties and impromptu comedy bits. Tozer patiently sat waiting for his turn "at-bat," as he later reflected. When he finally got to the pulpit, his first words were, "What has happened to you holiness people?" Scrapping his prepared sermon, he took that congregation to the "spiritual woodshed" like they had never been before.

Tozer believed that when believers gathered, they should cultivate the presence of Christ and honor the One who bore the shame and indignity of the cross for our sins. The Church was not a place to be silly or act crazy. These things were symptoms of the spiritual decline of the Church, and it concerned him greatly.

At times, Tozer's criticism could be rather sharp. For example, he once criticized a modern Bible translation by saying, "Reading that translation gave me the same feeling as I would get by shaving with a banana." When the translator heard the comment, he never quite forgave Tozer. Tozer was also extreme in his criticism of the religious movie and of churches that majored in "counting noses," but his criticism never came out of a heart of malice or a desire to make a name for himself. His primary concern was exalting Christ and reverencing His presence among the assembled believers. Consequently, there were those occasions when some were offended by his sharp criticisms.

During the last decade of his ministry, Tozer felt a particular burden for radical reformation within the evangelical Church. He sometimes referred to the evangelical Church as being in "Babylonian Captivity," and on many occasions he said he felt that the Church was giving in to the morals and values of the world around her. "We're in desperate need of a restoration," he often said.

Perhaps what concerned him the most was that the Church as he saw it was not the high, holy, Spirit-filled, fire-baptized,

God-conscious, humble, gracious and loving fellowship that the Church fathers had known in previous generations. "Until we have a Reformation," Tozer opined, "all of our books and our schools and our magazines are only the working of bacteria in the decaying Church."

To be fair, it was not Christianity that was changing but Christian leaders within Christianity. They were too much in the ways of the world, he believed. They often adopted the patterns of the business world of Madison Avenue for ministry and held the example of those holy ones who had gone on before in disdain. Pop-psychology had become more important than the plain teaching of the Bible. Tradition had become a bad word, and woe be to the minister who was referred to as "traditional." To Tozer, it seemed that Christianity was in the hands of those who wanted to be more like the world than like Christ.

On one occasion, Tozer had an opportunity to speak to a Youth for Christ leadership meeting, which also was being aired over the Moody radio network. He decided to take this opportunity to speak to the evangelical Church at large and, in his words, "nail his 13 thesis on the door of the evangelical Church." In the sermon, he bared his heart concerning the Reformation that he believed needed to happen within the evangelical Church.

Among the things he said in that sermon was that the way of the cross was hard. This was an important consideration on his part, because he felt that many people were trying to make the Christian life out to be an easy thing when the Scriptures showed how difficult it was to follow Jesus Christ. A Christian without the cross was unthinkable in his mind, and he believed that too many leaders were offering a brand of Christianity that was cheap and easy and did not lay the heavy burden of cross bearing on the people. This certainly was not the Christianity of the Church fathers, the reformers or the revivalists that had come before.

Tozer also emphasized the biblical truth that there can be no Savior without Lordship. His comments flew in the face of the idea that a person could accept Jesus Christ as Savior without accepting Him as the Lord of his or her life. That idea, according to Tozer, was a great fallacy within the evangelical Church. He emphasized as much as possible the fact that Jesus Christ is *both* Savior and Lord. There cannot be a divided Christ. To proclaim a divided Christ is to destroy the foundation of the Church.

Tozer criticized those churches that adopted the methods of the world in order to accomplish the agenda and goals of God. He pointed out three things that he believed were diametrically opposed to the work of the Holy Spirit in the local church: (1) the methods of big business, (2) the methods of show business, and (3) the methods of Madison Avenue advertisers. Along with this, he charged that the spirit of modern evangelism seemed to be foreign to that of the New Testament. By all costs, he believed that the Church must return to New Testament principles.

He also underscored that when Christ saves a person, He does so to make him or her both a worshiper *and* a worker. Tozer once said, "Unless we are worshipers we are simply religious Japanese dancing mice moving around in a circle getting nowhere."

A Call to Authentic Faith

Tozer's message was always consistent. He saw Christianity in turmoil and decline, and wherever he went he issued a clarion call for Christians to forsake the world and once again take up their crosses and follow Christ. What occupied much of his preaching and writing was the fact that he believed the Church needed to be restored to the New Testament pattern. He often said, "We have sold out to carnal methods, carnal philosophies, carnal viewpoints, carnal gadgets and have lost the glory of God in our midst. We're a starved generation that's never seen the glory of God."

When he spoke about this "Babylonian captivity" of the Church, he always emphasized two points: (1) believers need to have a desire for God's glory, and (2) they need to have a desire to experience His presence in reverent worship. Tozer said, "The glory of God has been lost to us in this day, and our God is a cheap God unworthy of our kneeling to." He tried to emphasize that the true God—the Father of Jesus Christ, the God of Abraham—is high and lifted up with His train filling the Temple (see Isa. 6:1).

Tozer saw the need to restore once again to the Church the lofty idea of who God really is. His passion was always to introduce the excellencies of the one called Christ to this generation of Christians. The effort to bring God down to a human level was absolutely anathema as far as he was concerned. The Church needed to get back again to reverent worship—worship deserving of God. He wanted to once again see church services in which the presence of God was so all-inspiring that you could not speak out loud; where the preaching of God was so high and lifted up that the people would go home in silence, unable to talk.

In *Reclaiming Christianity*, Tozer speaks out on these issues and many others that deal with the Church of Jesus Christ, especially the evangelical Church. He warns that we need to beware of what he called "the religious word game"—the belief many of us have that if we read something in the Bible, it must automatically be true in our lives. In one chapter, he discusses the idea that many good and powerful words used in the past have lost their meanings, or that many present-day leaders have changed the meanings of these words. He claims that these are "dead" words and are damaging the very core of Christianity. He then offers what he calls "live" words for present-day Christians and prays that the present generation of Christ-followers will become enflamed with the true meaning of authentic faith.

Tozer calls each of us to truly examine our hearts and stop simply playing at religion so that we can experience all that God has for us. God will give us everything that He has promised, but He will not give us anything He has *not* promised. In light of this, we need to search the Scriptures to see what God has indeed promised. Then, each of us can enter into the experience of that promise in our own hearts and lives, for the Christian life is not automatic but rather a life of discipline, self-denial and sacrifice.

As you read *Reclaiming Christianity*, you may not always agree with Tozer— He would not have wanted that anyway—but your faith will be challenged. It is my hope that this challenge will drive you to your Bible, and then to your knees.

A Call to Authentic Faith

1

CHRIST IS LORD OVER HIS CHURCH

And Jesus came and spake unto them, saying,
All power is given unto me in heaven and in earth.

MATTHEW 28:18

Therefore let all the house of Israel know assuredly,
that God hath made that same Jesus, whom ye
have crucified, both Lord and Christ.

ACTS 2:36

Before considering the Church in all of its aspects, we must clearly establish the foundation of the authority of the Church. If the Church had simply evolved over time, and Church doctrine and practice was merely a result of that evolution instead of an institution purposefully established by Christ, then we would have a different matter on our hands. However, this is not the case. There is an absolute authority within the Church, and that authority is Jesus Christ. This Christ is the Lord of His Church, and He will be the Lord of the world. How does Christ exercise His Lordship over the local church? The answer to this question solves a myriad of problems that are plaguing the evangelical Church today.

One way that Christ exercised His authority was by inspiring His apostles to write letters, as the Holy Spirit moved them, to the various churches. Much of the New Testament is comprised of these epistles. In Paul's letters, the apostle instructed new believers in doctrine and set forth authoritative injunctions to correct any wrong beliefs they had. These new churches, born out of raw paganism and baptized into the Body of Christ, had a desperate need for instruction. Nothing in their culture had enabled them to be what Christ had called them to be. They came out of paganism, and their gods had been the gods of pagans. Although they knew almost nothing of God and Christ, they believed on Christ, and now the Lord of the Church, through men like Paul who wrote to these churches explaining His truth.

Timeless Biblical Principles

Some Christians panic as soon as any problem arises in their church. Somebody gets offended, and the dear sensitive saints hold up their hands and run for cover, crying, "Isn't this just terrible?" But problems in the Church are nothing new, and there are really no new problems. The men of God who wrote the epistles had to deal with people who were offended. They wrote letters as they were inspired by the Holy Spirit to address these problems at a particular time in history, but in so doing they also solved them for all of us down through the ages. They laid down universally applicable principles, for there are as many problems in the Church as there are people.

It's a fact that some Christians are troubled. They are not optimistic, but pessimistic, and when they become Christians, they carry that pessimism over. A person carries his or her temperament into the kingdom of God. If you are bright, you carry that over into the Kingdom, and if you are a gloomy fellow, you carry that over as well. The point is, temperament is not sin, it is just the way a person is; and when he or she is converted, the Lord has to deliver that person from what is wrong in his or her temperament.

Our Lord is the same today as He was yesterday. His Church is also the same today as it was yesterday, so He does the same things today that He did before the New Testament canon was closed in the first two centuries. In Paul's day, thousands upon thousands of people lived in Rome, and tens of thousands lived in Corinth, Galatia, Thessalonica and Ephesus. There were hundreds of thousands of people, and yet the epistles say, "Paul, to the Romans." Why did Paul write to the Romans or to the Corinthians? He was not writing to the masses at all, but to the small minority group within Rome or Corinth. He was writing to those who had believed in the Lord Jesus Christ.

Paul addressed his epistles to a peculiar people within the community of those cities—a minority group identified as "the Church" who called Jesus Christ Lord and prayed to Him as God. In this way, Jesus addressed Himself to His own followers—the Christian community within a local city, a local church. He does the same today. He applies the inspired epistles to the situations we face every day. The epistles are for people who have heard about this Son of the virgin who came from God and died for men, who rose the third day, who opened the kingdom of heaven to believers, and who is now sitting at the right hand of God. They were written for people who have heard about Him and have come together, believed and worshiped.

When the apostles wrote their epistles, they wrote out of the authority of divine inspiration. Therefore, the epistles do not advise; they command. So these prescripts—these orders from Jesus Christ, the Head of the Church—come to us within the Church. For us today, they call us back to our first love. We have no other command or authority.

The epistles addressed those careless Christians who needed to be instructed and warned and cautioned. These Christians had to be corrected, for some of them were in error. For example, some had the wrong ideas about the resurrection of the dead, so Paul wrote 1 Corinthians 15 and put them straight on that issue. And some of them believed the Lord had already come, so Paul wrote 1 Thessalonians and put them straight on those faulty beliefs.

Even a man full of the Holy Spirit may allow the cares of this life to dull his spiritual life, causing him to neglect his prayer life and lose out in his spiritual life. Nothing God can do for you now can fix you like concrete so that you will always be good. You have to walk with God on a daily and continuous basis. That is what the epistles address.

Dealing with Carnality

It might be hard to imagine that there were carnal Christians even in the apostles' day. A carnal Christian has the seed of God in him, but he also holds on to the sins of lust and jealousy and many other things from the old life. Those evil things are described as "carnal," from the Latin word meaning "flesh." The carnal man, while he is born again, has so much of the old carnal nature that he is not living a very good life. So the Holy Spirit wrote, through the apostles, to men such as these. They had to be delivered from the sins of the flesh. What applied to them applies to us today.

There were also contentious, rebellious and divisive people in the Early Church, and their numbers have not decreased today. The Lord wrote to them and to us, through His apostles, to straighten us out. The Holy Spirit worked through Paul to lay a theological foundation. He told the believers how things were so that they might be encouraged and hear the exhortation that followed.

It is surprising how many Christians live below the scriptural expectation for their lives. They are gloomy. They wake up in the morning and think for a moment that everything they knew and thought they had in Christ, and all that they thought God had done for them, was a mistake. Maybe later on they find their way through, but for a while they are discouraged. Some people are like that, so the Lord has to encourage them. Some Christians are born into the world as bouncing Christian babies, and others are thin and anemic and have a long, hard time of it. So the Holy Spirit has something to say to all people.

The Holy Spirit, through the Scriptures, lets people know what they can have and what they cannot have. And if we are faithful to tell them what we believe and what God can offer them, they will come to us and say, "How can I get in on what you have?"

The Mystery of Reconciliation

Here is what the Scriptures state that we are to tell the people: "Therefore if any man be in Christ, he is a new creature: old things are passed away; behold, all things are become new" (2 Cor. 5:17). That word "creature" is the right one there. He is a new creature, a new creation, and all things are of God who has reconciled us to Himself by Jesus Christ.

What is reconciliation? Reconciliation occurs when two enemies come together in love. God, who is the enemy of sin, and man, who is the enemy of God, were reconciled together in Jesus Christ. And when Jesus, who is God *and* man, died on the cross for man, He brought the two together through the mystery of reconciliation.

Note that it was not man who reconciled himself to God, but God who reconciled Himself to man. And through that act He has given us the ministry of reconciliation "to wit, that God was in Christ, reconciling the world unto himself, not imputing their trespasses unto them; and hath committed unto us the word of reconciliation" (2 Cor. 5:19).

Note that God did not say, "You will be reconciled if you *feel* reconciled. He said, "If any man be in Christ, he is a new creature"; he *has been* reconciled. And if you experience reconciliation, you will want to go out and tell someone else about it. That is evangelism at the grass roots. Evangelism in depth, you might call it now.

Here's another admonition from the Holy Spirit through the apostle Paul: "Giving thanks unto the Father, which hath made us meet to be partakers of the inheritance of the saints in light: who hath delivered us from the power of darkness, and hath translated us into the kingdom of his dear Son: in whom we have redemption through his blood, even the forgiveness of sins" (Col. 1:12-14).

God has made us worthy to be partakers of the inheritance of the saints in the light. There is no apostle Paul, Frances of Assisi or saint anywhere that has any more right than we have. "If any man be in Christ, he is a new creature"; he has been reconciled, and God has made him to be a partaker of the inheritance of the saints in light "who hath delivered us from the power of darkness, and hath translated us into the kingdom of His dear Son." Now there is a translation I believe in: the translation out of the kingdom of darkness.

When you hear of the terrible things men are doing, do you wonder why? It is because they are under the power of darkness. But when they hear about this virgin's Son—this wonderful, mysterious man who came from the world above and who reconciled us to God—and they believe, they are delivered from that darkness and are translated into the kingdom of the Son of His love.

This is what happened when you were converted. You were made worthy to be a partaker in the inheritance. You were not worthy, but God made you worthy; and when God makes anybody worthy, it is so. You have been forgiven, so act like it. "What God hath cleansed, that call not thou unclean" (Acts 11:8). If God cleanses you of anything, you do no one any good by lying down like a whipped spaniel. So get up and thank God that you have been made worthy to be one of His children, delivered out of the power of darkness, and redeemed through His blood.

Chosen and Blessed

In Ephesians 1:3, Paul writes, "Blessed be the God and Father of our Lord Jesus Christ, who hath blessed us with all spiritual blessings in heavenly places in Christ." Some people think that a "heavenly place" is a church, but the word "places" in verse 3 should not be in the English translation. The word Greek word for "heavenly" is actually plural; it means "heavenlies" in the realm of the Spirit and of heavenly things. Thus, what Paul is saying is that God has blessed us with all spiritual blessings in the heavenlies. He has already done this. He has blessed us with all spiritual blessings in the heavenlies, in Christ, just as "he hath chosen us in him before the foundation of the world" (v. 4).

God is eternal and has already lived all of our days. He is at the end of time as well as the beginning, for time is simply a little incident on the bosom of God. God surrounds time and has already lived all the tomorrows. Back before time was, God saw you, knew who you would be and knew what your name would be. He knew how tall you would be, whether you would be a man or woman, whether you would be married or single. He knew whether you would be American or German or Japanese. He knew all about you, smiled and laid His hand on you.

You say, "Oh, but why didn't I know it sooner?"

It is a mystery, but I do know this: You would never have come to Him if He had not turned to you. Do not ever get up, stick your chest out and say, "I sought the Lord." You sought the Lord after He made it tough for you and pushed you and urged you. He is the aggressor, not you.

You did not do anything but respond, and the Lord had to get behind you and push. That is the way all God's people came to Him, so do not feel bad about it. And He chose you before the foundation of the world. God knew your name and my name before there was a sea or a mountain, before there was a star or a planet.

Accepted in the Beloved

Again, through the apostle Paul, we are admonished, "That we should be holy and without blame before him in love; having predestinated us unto the adoption of children" (Eph. 1:4). What does "predestinated" mean? Well, "pre" means "before," and "destinated" means "to choose a destination or destiny." Beforehand, He determined your destiny. And what is the Christian's destiny? It is to be made by Jesus Christ for Himself. And why did He do it? "According to the good pleasure of his will." God wanted to do it. God said, "If I wanted to do that, you need not worry about it. What is that to you? I wanted to do it."

It is out of the good pleasure of God's will and it is "to the praise of the glory of his grace, wherein he hath made us accepted in the beloved" (v. 6). No one can come straight to God and be accepted. A Christian is one who believes the truth that there is only one door and that door is the Son of God Himself. We are only accepted in the Beloved. That is why I cannot go along with these nature poets, these religious poets and all these strange people who teach how you can come to God anywhere and in any way. "There is nothing unique about Christianity," they say. According to them, God has spoken to Greeks, to Plato, to the Muslim in Mohammed and the Buddhist in Buddha. Let anybody believe what he wants to.

That is not Christianity, and that is not what the Bible teaches. Anybody who thinks he is still a Christian and teaches that has been educated beyond his intelligence and needs to start over. The simple fact is that there is only one way: "No man cometh unto the Father, but by me" (John 14:6). You cannot walk straight out of the woods into heaven. You come by the only door there is, Jesus Christ the Lord. But thank God, that door is as wide as you need.

The Spirit also encourages us in Romans 5:1, "Therefore being justified by faith, we have peace with God through our Lord Jesus Christ." This peace is not what everybody is running after and taking pills to get. You will never get it in a bottle. God did not say, "Being justified by grace, you have peace of heart." He said you have "peace with God."

The man who is under sentence of death does not have peace with the state. When a magistrate has a man stand up trembling before him and says, "I'm sorry to have to do this, but the testimony of witnesses and the laws of this dominion require me to say that you shall be kept in such and such a jail until such and such a date and then hang by the neck until dead." There is a scream in the courtroom as his relatives hear it, and he turns gray, tries to smile at his lawyer and is led away. There is no peace in his heart, but that is not what I mean.

And so, there was hostility between God and man. Man had sinned, violated the laws of God and incurred death, and the soul that sins shall die. There was no peace between man and his God. Then came Jesus and opened the kingdom of heaven to all who would believe, and now therefore being justified by faith, we have peace with God. The high court of heaven is no longer angry with us and no longer says we must die but declares that we may live.

The Outcome of Tribulation

Now, do not think that God does not give you peace of heart as well. I do not mean to leave that impression, but that is not what we are talking about here. We have access by faith into this grace and we "rejoice in hope of the glory of God. And not only so, but we glory in tribulations also: knowing that tribulation worketh patience" (Rom. 5:3).

We say, "O, God, give me patience." God does not give us patience as we might go and buy a can of beans at the grocery store. He gives us patience by letting us suffer tribulations. Nobody likes that. We say, "Lord, I wish I could do it differently." But God knows best, after all. If He put tribulation before you and said He will give you patience by giving you a little trouble along the way, wouldn't you take a little trouble?

You say, "Lord, I want all my highways paved." The Lord says, "I'm sorry, I can't accommodate you. I'm going to let you run over some bumps occasionally, so you will have patience." You do not like the bumps, but you like the patience, and if you want the patience, you will have to take the bumps. And what is patience but experience?

The Holy Spirit offers a word for young, scared and troubled Christians: "Who shall separate us from the love of Christ? Shall tribulation, or distress, or persecution, or famine, or nakedness, or peril, or sword? As it is written, For thy sake we are killed all the day long . . . for I am persuaded, that neither death, nor life, nor angels, nor principalities, nor powers, nor things present, nor things to come, Nor height, nor depth, nor any other creature, shall be able to separate us from the love of God, which is in Christ Jesus our Lord" (Rom. 8:35-36,38-39).

Free Indeed!

All right, Christian, if you are truly born again and truly love Christ, do you see where that puts you? Do you see that you are something new in the universe, something different in the population? You are a privileged and honored person, you are rich and under God, you are wonderful. Therefore, you ought to thank Him and continue to thank Him.

That deep inward defeat can be cured only by an equal inward release. When the Lord releases a man, he is free; and until he is released, you cannot sing him free, you cannot pound him free, you cannot preach him free and you cannot get him free any way known to mortal man. Yet the Church spends millions of dollars every year putting on religious stuff in order to try to get people free. One simple act of the Holy Spirit will free a man; free him forever and turn him loose. And you can go to God and get bold about it.

When I was young, I got in some kind of inward jam. The burden was on me, and I felt bound and miserable. One day, I was walking along the street in west Akron, Ohio, and I had had enough. I knew that God was not mad at me, and I knew the devil was bothering me. Suddenly, I stopped, stamped my foot in bold daylight, looked up through the trees to God and said, "God, I won't stand this anymore." And I didn't. Right then, I became a free man. That particular thing left me. God set me free, because He knew it took faith. I was not mad at the Lord;

I was mad at the devil. And it was not the Lord that had me bound; it was the old devil.

I believe the Lord's people could be a happier people, and then more souls would be converted. "Restore unto me the joy of thy salvation . . . then will I teach transgressors thy ways; and sinners shall be converted unto thee" (Ps. 51:12-13). It always follows that a church that is happy from the inside out did not have to pay a dime to be happy, did not have to import anything to find happiness. It was there already. That would be a sample of a New Testament Church.

It is possible to have a logjam in a church. One or two logs get crossed, somebody gets offended, and the work of God cannot go on. But the Holy Spirit is wonderfully able to find logjams and release them. The preacher does not know; he is as innocent as a newborn babe in arms. But the Holy Spirit knows, and so He finds that person. And if He can get the co-operation of the fellow that has the issue, away it goes and the blessing of God comes.

Jesus Christ exercises absolute authority over the Scriptures written by men who were moved by the Holy Spirit. Every problem in the Church, from the day of Pentecost to this very hour, is addressed in that marvelous book we call the Word of God. If we are going to reclaim the Christianity of the New Testament, we must return to the faith of the New Testament.

2

THE RELEVANT AUTHORITY OF THE WORD OF GOD

And, Thou, Lord, in the beginning hast laid the foundation of the earth;
and the heavens are the works of thine hands: They shall perish;
but thou remainest; and they all shall wax old as doth a garment;
And as a vesture shalt thou fold them up, and they shall be changed:
but thou art the same, and thy years shall not fail.

HEBREWS 1:10-12

In the Church, supreme authority resides in God and in Him alone. This is emphatically declared in both the Old Testament and the New and has been the unanimous belief of Christians throughout the centuries. Nothing has changed to negate this in any degree.

God possesses supreme authority for certain reasons. He possesses supreme authority because of His eternity. *God was* before all authorities.

I do not say that there are not authorities; I well know there are. But God was before all authorities. Lords, kings, emperors and potentates have certain authority, but that authority is late in time and is borrowed from God, and therefore is temporary. And whatever is temporary cannot be final and supreme.

Then there is another kind of authority with prophets and apostles and popes and bishops and religious sages. If they are good, they have borrowed their authority; and if they are bad, they have usurped it. They have authority all right; nobody can doubt it.

Bishops have authority. They can say, "Don't you do so-and-so," and the little preacher does not dare do it. Then there are popes and apostles and prophets. Now I say again that if they were good men, they borrowed their authority from God; and if they were bad men, they usurped it from God. So either way they got it from God. But they all had to surrender their authority and die.

That is the oddest thing that those who admit it do not live as if they were going to die. But we are all just little boys that Mother Nature is going to put to bed one of these days. The little fellow has keyed himself up with excitement; he wants to stay up, and mother says, "No, you've got to go to bed, Junior."

And Junior says, "Oh, just a half hour yet, Mother."

"No, it's time now; in fact it's past time." And she says, "I've made up your bed and it's all ready now, and you go to bed."

He does not like it and fights it until he cannot keep his eyes open. Finally, he crawls in and goes to bed over his own protest. So it is with Mother Nature. She has all her boys; some of them just plain people like you and me with no particular mark of distinction. And then, of course, there are some who have the insignia of greatness. They wear on their shoulders or foreheads proof that they have some authority, and there they are—the king with his crown, the president with his constitution, the bishop with his hat, the cardinal with his red skullcap—playing with their toys. They all want to play with their toys, but Mother Nature pays no attention to how important they are when she says, "Go to bed now."

The Pope says, "No, I want to stay up a little while longer, Mother; I want to make some more inane speeches."

Mother Nature says, "No, go to bed now."

And the Bishop says, "No, I want to stay up and move my men around. I'm playing with my men. I want to stay and move my men some more."

Mother Nature says, "You've moved all the men you're going to move. Get off to bed now."

They all have to do it, and my contention is that anything you cannot keep cannot be final. You can have it for a little while but not for very long. We all surrender to man's final fate, which is death.

Over against the transitory, passing, relative and tentative authority of prophets, apostles, kings, popes, emperors, bishops and presidents, and all the rest, stands these awesome words: "Thou, Lord, in the beginning hast laid the foundation of the earth; and the heavens are the works of thine hands: they shall perish; but thou remainest; and they all shall wax old as doth a garment; and as a vesture shalt thou fold them up, and they shall be changed: but thou art the same, and thy years shall not fail" (Heb. 1:10-12). Before the world was, God was; and when the worlds have burnt themselves out, God will remain the supreme authority.

Some of God's attributes—love, kindness, compassion, pity, holiness and righteousness—He can share with His people. But there are other attributes so divine that God cannot share them. Self-existence, sovereignty, omniscience and all-wisdom—these declare God to have all the authority there is.

I once saw a cartoon in a religious magazine showing Martin Luther standing up with great dignity saying, "I can do nothing else; here I stand." Then it showed a whole herd of little creatures running toward Rome, saying, "Here we go." Luther said, "Here I stand," and they said, "Here we go." And as they go, they are trampling the 95 theses under their feet. I tell you, it is hard to stand and say, "Here I stand," but it is easy to follow the crowd. All you have to do is keep the holy neck of the pastor in sight just ahead of you. Keep right after him; pay no attention to where he is going.

God Almighty is a sovereign God because He is self-existent. He is sovereign. He is omniscient and He stands absolutely. It would be great if we Protestants would remember that now.

How God Utters His Authority

The Bible is a vehicle of God's authority. This book is called "the Book of"—the Book of the Lord, the Good Word of God, the Holy writings, the Law of the Lord, the Word of Christ, the Oracles of God, the Word of Life and the Word of Truth. These are descriptions of the Word through which God utters His authority. And this Word is said to be God-breathed, indestructible and eternal.

In the Word, we have that unique thing. This Book of the Lord, the uttered Word of God, is that unique thing that always ought to be spelled out in capitals. It is different from and above, and transcending all others of its kind. It is uncompromising, authoritative, awesome and eternal. And it is through this Word that God exercises His supreme, self-bestowed authority, for He never took His authority from men. The Lord never kneeled before anyone who touched His shoulder with a sword and said, "Rise, sovereign God." There is nobody who can bestow sovereignty upon the sovereign God.

"The word that I have spoken," said Jesus, "the same shall judge him in the last day" (John 12:48). Is it any wonder then that the prophet says, "O earth, earth, earth, hear the word of the LORD" (Jer. 22:29). God's uttered Word, this is what we have here, and it is through God's uttered Word that He exercises His authority. He utters Himself forth. It is the nature of God to express Himself. And so He utters Himself forth, and what He utters originates in the mind of an infinite Creator and comes to the mind of a finite creature.

Some people are so ponderously intellectual that the idea that God speaks to man bothers them. But it does not bother me at all. I believe that the infinite God can speak to finite man. I do not believe there is any bridge that cannot be crossed when the infinite Creator determines that He is going to utter forth His authoritative Word to finite man. He can do it; and in this uttered Word is sovereign authority *with the power of life and death.* That is not too strong an expression. The Scripture declares it to be so, that the gospel is the Word of life, and the day will come when every "t" will be crossed and every "i" will be dotted, and there will not be one iota of God's mighty Word which will not come to pass.

There is a beautiful expression taken not from the sacred Scriptures but from that which is very close. It bears the same relation to the holy, inspired, unique thing that a good devotional book bears to the New Testament. I refer to the Wisdom of Solomon. There, he says this about the Word of God: "For while all things were in quiet silence, and that night was in the midst of her swift course, Thine Almighty word leaped down from heaven out of thy royal throne, as a fierce man of war into the midst of a land of destruction, and brought thine unfeigned commandment as a sharp sword, and standing up filled all things with death; and it touched the heaven, but it stood upon the earth" (Wisdom 18:14-16).

When I read it, I marked the words "Thine almighty word leaped down from heaven," for it dramatizes the way the Word came to man from the royal throne that never was built because it was always there. The throne upon which sits the Almighty God. And this Word comes down like a fierce man of war into the midst of the land of destruction.

That is why I do not like to see man tinker with the Word of God. That is why I do not like to see editors, annotators and translators who, in irreverence and carelessness, and sometimes for money, make up new translations. This Almighty Word leaped down from the royal throne, and I have to be careful because it is that unique will of God revealed to me. It is God uttering forth His sovereign authority through printed words that I can get hold of.

These words are said to be lively, dynamic and creative. When God spoke, it was done; and when He commanded it, it stood forth, and creation came by His Word. For that we should never think of God as getting down on His knees and working on a piece of clay like a potter. All that is beautiful figure, but the fact is, God spoke back in the first chapters of Genesis. "And God said, let there be light: and there was light . . . And God said let the earth bring forth . . . and it was so" (Gen. 1:3,11). And whatever God said, happened. There will be a day when we will see that every word that God speaks will come to pass. This Almighty Word that leaped down from heaven out of the royal throne is a fierce man-o-war filled with life, and dynamic with created power. And God is creating new men through the truth. The day will be when Jesus Christ will call all the nations before Him, and He will do it by His Word.

Life and Death in the Word

God's Word is both our terror and our hope. God's Word both kills and makes alive. If we engage it in faith, humility and obedience, it gives life and it cleanses, feeds and defends. If we will close it in unbelief, ignore it or resist it, it will accuse us before the God who gave it, for it is the living Word of God. We dare not resist it nor argue it down.

Some people believe part of the Word but do not believe the other part. They say, "If it inspires me, it is inspired; and if it does not inspire me, it is simply old history and tradition." I believe this is God's unique thing—the uttered Word of the living God—and when we get into the meaning of it and know what God is uttering forth, it has power to kill those who resist and it has power to make alive those who believe. "The LORD hath made bare his holy arm in the eyes of all the nations. . . . Who hath believed our report? And to whom is the arm of the LORD revealed?" (Isa. 52:10; 53:1). Unbelief will paralyze the arm of the man who is filled with unbelief. While that same arm, long from being paralyzed, is working for the salvation of men.

Where can we see this awesome power of the Word of God? Years ago, missionaries went to some pyramid mountain or some other location in a Stone-age culture in Irian Jaya. For a long time they thought these people would not be converted at all; they thought that nobody there even knew the Word of God or ever knew there was a God.

When the missionaries first went there they said, "We come to you preaching God, your Creator." And the natives said, "We're not created, we came up out of the river." According to their tradition, they came up out of the river. Yet they were too busy killing each other to sit down and ask who made the river.

The missionary went to work on a language never before reduced to writing. They had no grammar and no lexicon, dictionary or list of words. Patiently the missionary sat around by the hour, cupping his ear while getting them to talk. He listened carefully to the diversity of sound and then put the word down. That is how they got the word "money" and the word for "God"—by listening.

Then they begin preaching the gospel of Jesus at last. After all these thousands of years, they uttered forth God's sovereign Word in the guttural language of the all-but-subhuman Dani tribe. Because of the Word of God being preached, the Dani have believed in Jesus Christ, are being converted and are walking in the light the best they know. Instead of the filthy sex songs of the days gone by, they are now singing the best they can. They know nothing about music. They sang simply by imitating what they heard and they are now singing the songs of Zion and getting the mighty Word of God. God's Word is a strong word, a unique thing; there is power in it. And when I believe it and engage it, and it engages me, something happens: the eternal God does an eternal act.

God's authoritative Word sounds in warning and invitation.

A Word of Warning

Go to your Bible and you will hear God give such warnings as, "the soul that sinneth, it shall die" (Ezek. 18:4). And, "the wicked shall be turned into hell, and all the nations that forget God" (Ps. 9:17). And, "that soul shall be cut off from among his people" (Exod. 31:14). And, "except a man be born again, he cannnot see the kingdom of God" (John 3:3). And, "except ye repent, ye shall all likewise perish" (Luke 13:3). And, "not every one that saith unto me, Lord, Lord, shall enter into the kingdom of heaven; but he that doeth the will of my Father" (Matt. 7:21). And, "no whoremonger, nor unclean person, nor covetous man, who is an idolater, hath any inheritance in the kingdom of God" (Eph. 5:5). Those are the awful words of God. He is speaking forth this unique thing in this authoritative utterance.

Nobody dares rise and say, "Let us explain this in the light of what Plato said." I do not care what Plato said. I have read Plato off and on, but I do not care what Plato says when God says, "the soul that sinneth shall die." Let Plato kneel before the authoritative Word of God. God has spoken His authority through His Word; let no Pope rise and say, "We'll explain that in the light of what Father So-and-so said." Let Father So-and-so be still. His mouth will soon be stuffed with dust. And let everybody keep still while God Almighty speaks. "O earth, earth, earth, hear the word of the LORD" (Jer. 22:29). "Hear, O heavens, and give ear, O earth: for the LORD hath spoken" (Isa. 1:2).

A Word of Invitation

There is also beautiful invitation in the Word of God. This is not the result of a group of religious people meeting together, having a board meeting and deciding that they are to say it. No, God Almighty said it. He spoke it out of heaven; it leaped down as a strong man in the night and filled the earth with a sound of His voice.

And God says, "If you will turn unto the Me, then I will have mercy upon you." And the Word of the Lord says, "Come unto me, all ye that labour and are heavy laden, and I will give you rest" (Matt. 11:28). And the Word of the Lord says, "If thou shalt confess with thy mouth the Lord Jesus, and shalt believe in thine heart that God hath raised him from the dead, thou shalt be saved" (Rom. 10:9). And it says, "By grace are ye saved through faith; and that not of yourselves" (Eph. 2:8) and, "If we confess our sins, he is faithful and just to forgive us our sins, and to cleanse us from all unrighteousness" (1 John 1:9). Here is the authoritative voice that needs no editing, no interrupting, no explaining; it only needs to be released.

Charles H. Spurgeon, the preacher from London, was invited once to come and give a series of 10 lectures in defense of the Bible. He wired back, "I will not come, the Bible needs no defense." Turn it loose, and like a lion, it will defend itself. I believe that, and I believe the Word of God needs no defense. We only need to preach it.

We are on our haunches now, fighting a rearguard action before the Neo-Orthodoxy and Liberals and the World Council of Churches and the new idea of a monolithic church with Poppa at the top. We are on our haunches now, but I pay no attention to any of them. The great God Almighty has spoken, and when He has spoken, let the world be silent and listen, for God has said it and God will fulfill all His warnings and of His invitations.

In the book of Luke there is that terrible passage, "the rich man also died, and was buried; and in hell he lift up his eyes, being in torments, and seeth Abraham afar off, and Lazarus in his bosom" (Luke 16:22-23). The rich man who had fared sumptuously had suddenly stopped faring sumptuously and was now in hell begging for a drop of water for his parched tongue. He became an evangelist, and he said, "Abraham, if you will not help me, please help my five brothers; for I have five brothers back home who are not believers, and if you will send Lazarus maybe he can save them . . . maybe they'll repent."

Abraham answered, "No, he can't cross over."

The rich man pleaded like an evangelist and said, "Please Abraham, won't you send him to my five brothers? I neglected them while I lived; now I want to help them. Send him please, for if somebody rises from the dead, they'll hear him."

"If they will not hear the Word," Abraham answered, "they will not believe though one rose from the dead" (see Luke 16:26-31).

If you have it in your heart to resist this unique thing, this uttered voice of the Almighty God, this authority that commands and invites, then if we had a graveyard rise and everybody in it rose—all the way back to the founding fathers—and began to preach, your heart would still be hard. For the Scripture says, "If they will not hear the word they will not hear the dead when they rise."

Some people ask me what they should read. Most of the Bible is written in the masculine gender, and many women just say that it means mankind, and that means men. But I have a text for women in the fifty-fourth chapter of Isaiah: "For thy Maker is thine husband; the LORD of hosts is his name; and thy Redeemer the Holy One of Israel; the God of the whole earth shall he be called. For the LORD hath called thee as a woman forsaken and grieved in spirit, and a wife of youth, when thou wast refused, saith thy God. For a small moment have I forsaken thee; but with great mercies will I gather thee" (Isa. 54:5-7).

In all the parliaments of the world, with all their wisdom, they cannot say anything that has meant so much to the human race as these words. All of the congresses down in Washington D.C., in the course of one whole century, cannot add up to as much as what is in these words. "For a small moment have I forsaken thee; but with great mercies will I gather thee. In a little wrath I hid my face from thee for a moment; but with everlasting kindness will I have mercy on thee, saith the LORD thy Redeemer" (Isa. 54:7-8). There it is. There is your hope, there is your hiding place, there is your rock, there is your future, there is your glory.

God is speaking authoritatively. Nobody has any right to come in and say, "I do not believe that."

God's Redeeming Covenant

The Word of the living God still sounds through the world, destroying what it does not redeem. And in that awful day when God shakes all that can be shaken, that living, vibrant, awesome, awful, powerful eternal Word will destroy all that it cannot redeem. I, for my part, want to be on the side of the redeemed.

Many times I get down on my knees here in the fifty-fourth chapter of Isaiah and let this unique thing speak to my heart. I hear that Word saying—a voice that goes clear to the depths of my being—"For this is as the waters of Noah unto me: for as I have sworn that the waters of Noah should no more go over the earth; so have I sworn that I would not be wroth with thee, nor rebuke thee" (v. 9). The great God who did not need to swear anything swore by Himself that He would not be wroth with me nor rebuke me. And in my own room, I put my name in there and repeat it with all my three names: Aiden Wilson Tozer. "For the mountains shall depart, and the hills be removed; but my kindness shall not depart from thee, neither shall the covenant of my peace be removed" (v. 10).

Nobody can take away the kindness of God from the people that are seeking; they cannot remove the covenant of God's saving grace from the man that trusts in Him when the mountain moves. The mountains are no more and then it cannot be for God said He will not move that mercy, for the mercy of God remains eternal and forever and forever. These are the words of God.

I believe this authority is relevant for me today. I do not go to priests, pastors, bishops or doctors. I go to God and to His Son, Jesus Christ.

O Word of God Incarnate
By William W. How (1823-1897)

O Word of God incarnate,
O wisdom from on high,
O truth unchanged, unchanging,
O light of our dark sky;
We praise Thee for the radiance
That from the hallowed page,
A lantern to our footsteps,
Shines on from age to age.

The church from her dear Master
Received the gift divine,
And still that light she lifteth
O'er all the earth to shine.
It is the golden casket
Where gems of truth are stored;
It is the heav'n-drawn picture
Of Christ, the living Word.

It floateth like a banner
Before God's host unfurled;
It shineth like a beacon
Above the darkling world.
It is the chart and compass
That o'er life's surging sea,
'Mid mists and rocks and quicksands,
Still guides, O Christ, to Thee.

O make Thy church, dear Savior,
A lamp of purest gold,
To bear before the nations
Thy true light as of old.
O teach Thy wand'ring pilgrims
By this their path to trace,
Till, clouds and darkness ended,
They see Thee face to face. Amen.

3

THIS THING CALLED CHRISTENDOM

*Then said Jesus to those Jews which believed on him, If ye continue in
my word, then are ye my disciples indeed; And ye shall know the truth,
and the truth shall make you free.*

JOHN 8:31-32

We have established the authority of the Church and that it has
a reason for being; now we need to consider the Church in its
broadest terms. The word "church" means many things to different people; this thing we call Christendom is composed of
believers all over the world.

The Jews living in Jesus' time were said to be believers. But
the conversation Jesus had with them indicated they were very
far off the track. Here is where they were off the track: They were
in physical descent from Abraham and proud of it. And our
Lord did not deny it. He said, "I know that ye are Abraham's
seed" (John 8:37). Their error was not in believing that they
were physically descended from Abraham, but that they were
automatically the spiritual descendants of Abraham. And our
Lord tried to explain this to them. I do not think they got it.

He said, "If ye were Abraham's children, ye would do the works of Abraham" (v. 39).

Christ did not reckon internal life and external conduct by physical descent. He took the Pharisees out of the covenant and said, "You are not true sons of Abraham, you are not children of Abraham at all, you are a seed of Abraham. You are the descendants of Abraham but you are not his children, because Abraham was a man of humility, obedience, faith and love, and you are none of these things. You hate me because I tell you the truth; you want to kill me for no fault but preaching truth to you, this did not Abraham." I am not dealing here with Abraham and the Jews but with this thing we call Christendom. In addition to the cults, it is composed of Roman Catholics, Greek Orthodox, Protestant liberals and evangelicals.

The word "evangelical" is to be thought of in lowercase letters. I am not referring to the Evangelical church—the denomination. I am referring to us and others like us. We also compose Christendom—we who are Bible-believing evangelicals, the Pentecostals in various shades and intensities of heat, the holiness people, the deeper life people, the victorious life people and the good old Calvinistic fundamentalists.

Evangelicals are a little guilty of an error that is not quite so tragically bad as the Pharisees', but it is an error nonetheless. We assume, and rather proudly, and without any proof, that we are in direct lineal descent from the apostles.

The Jews in Jesus' day assumed this. Anything you are not sure of and have to argue yourself into is sin. But when you are so confident of it that you do not even mention it, that is worse. And until our Lord pressed them, the Pharisees did not even mention it. They took for granted that they were the descendants of Abraham, and that all Abraham had, they had.

We evangelicals rule out the Roman Catholics without hesitation; we rule out the Greek Orthodox and the Protestant liberals. However, when it comes to Bible-believing evangelicals such as we are, we rule ourselves in. We imagine and believe that we are in descent, in spiritual succession, from the apostles, from our Lord and His apostles and from the Early Church.

Just as the Jews were in physical descent from Abraham, and nobody challenged this, so the evangelicals are in creedal descent from the apostles. We believe the same thing that Paul believed, the same thing that Peter and John and the man who wrote the Book of Hebrews and the Book of Acts believed. We evangelicals believe what they believed. We do not doubt it at all. We believe the Word of God.

We are in creedal descent from the apostles. Nobody is going to challenge that. The error is in assuming that because we are in creedal descent, we are in spiritual succession. The Pharisees made that mistake, and the Lord straightened them out and quietly ruled them out of Abraham's covenant. It is entirely possible that we are assuming too much as well. Because we believe what Paul believed, we assume, therefore, that we have all that Paul had. Because we believe what Peter believed, therefore, we are all that Peter was. Because we are in creedal conformity, we assume that we are also spiritually identical.

This we dare not do. I think of the little song's lyrics, "with eternity's values in view." That is what I try to do, and therefore, I do not want to take anything for granted. That is why I don't like preachers who paw me over and smooth me down and make me feel good whether I'm good or not. If I am not good, I do not want to feel good. That is a terrible trap. If I am not good, I want to feel natural. I want to know the truth about myself.

If we support our claim to be in living succession from the apostles, then we have to show that "this" which we are is "that" which they were. Jesus disproved the claims and assumptions of the Jews, saying, "This did not Abraham." He said, "This that you have is not that, which Abraham had." This is not "that," and this "did not Abraham"; Jesus ruled them out.

Marks of True Spiritual Identity

There is only one real spiritual succession from the apostles—the New Testament Church fathers. The proof of such spiritual succession is identity with them. If we can point to ourselves and say, "This," and then point to the New Testament Church and say, "is that," and make it stick, then we ought to be the happiest people in the world; and we have reason for being happy. If I can point to the evangelical church and say, "This is that," and then point to Paul and the rest of them as the "that," then we have the "this." If you are the same, then we are not wrong in our assumptions. But what if there is a difference, as there was between the Jews and Abraham? Jesus said, "Abraham was not like you. You claim to be of spiritual descent from Abraham—you claim to carry on the spiritual succession—but you are going one way and Abraham was going another."

I want to offer some indications necessary to prove that "this" is "that" and show that we are in spiritual descent from the apostles, and that what we have among us today is truly the New Testament Church.

What are the marks that identify our relationship to the Early Church?

Attitude Toward Doctrinal Creed

The first mark is *creedal identification*—creedal proof of identification with the Early Church. We must believe what they believed and think that it is possible to be a good Christian without leaving the truth. We should not be off on anything; we should, as they did, believe the entire Bible.

I never did enough thinking or got enough education ever to jar my belief in the whole Scripture. I get happy about the Scriptures like some people get worried about them. I read them, usually in the *King James Version,* though I have 25 or 30 other versions, and I just believe them.

It can be proved by any man of goodwill that the doctrinal position of the evangelical Church today is identical with the doctrinal position of the Church fathers. The evangelical Church is, in fact, in creedal descent from those on the day of Pentecost.

This is the first proof.

Attitude Toward Morality

The second mark of identification is an *identity of moral elevation.* The moral standards of the evangelical Church today must be the same as the apostolic Church. After all, nothing has changed, and man with all his improvements is still but a man.

The evangelical Church ought to have a height of moral elevation so great that the sinners look up there. Instead of that, we have edited it down, watered it down and diluted it. We have people showing us that we ought not to be holier than thou, but that we ought to say, "We are the same as you, only we have a Savior."

This would be like two men dying on hospital beds in the same ward and one saying to the other, "I have what you have but the only difference between us is that I have a physician and you don't."

You could not interest a dying man in another man who is so well off because he had a physician. If the physician could not cure the fellow, what was the good of the physician? He might as well be out playing golf.

If I go to a sinner and say, "I am exactly the same as you, the only difference is that I have a Savior," but I do all the same things he does—I tell the same dirty jokes he tells and I waste my time the same way he does and I do everything he does—and then I say, "I have a Savior, you ought to have a Savior," doesn't he have the right to ask me what kind of Savior I have? What profit is there for a man to say, "I have a physician" if he is dying on a cot? What does it profit a man to say, "I have a Savior" if he is living in iniquity?

The church of Jesus Christ in apostolic days had a very high moral elevation. If any church does not have a level of moral elevation comparable to the New Testament church, then it has violated the law of spiritual succession and it may be in doctrinal and lineal descent from the apostles but morally it has broken its succession and pulled out.

Attitude Toward God

The next point of identification is our *attitude toward God*. The Early Church believed in the triune God—the Father, the Son and the Holy Spirit. Not only did they believe Him according to a creed, but He was everything to them. God was at the center of their life; they gathered unto the Lord; they worshiped the Lord; they obeyed the Lord; and the Lord was everything to them.

Sadly, in some churches, God is no longer necessary. Some churches claim to believe in God but by way of doctrine have it so arranged at their church that God is not necessary to them for success. To the average church, God is desirable and may even be useful, but He is not necessary. Most churches can get on without God; they just give God His place in a nice way, as a guest. They say, "Our honored guest is here tonight," but He is soon forgotten in the midst of all the claptrap. That is not an apostolic church.

I pray often—and I want to live in line with my prayer—that God puts me in a state where He has to help me or I will flop. I want to be in a place where I have to have God in everything that I do.

I like to be in a place where God is indispensable to me. I would like to be where Elijah was when he teased those prophets of Baal (see 1 Kings 18:16-38). Those prophets had cut themselves all day and were angry, and Baal had not heard them. Elijah needled them, "Your God is asleep, he's hunting or he's off in conversation with someone." He said, "Baal will hear you, Baal will hear you after awhile." When he got them so mad that they were in a state of frustration and bitterness, it came time for him to offer his offerings.

If God had not helped Elijah, those prophets of Baal would have torn him from limb to limb. It was not a question of, "Now, Father, we thank You. You're here and we're here, amen."

But Elijah said, "God, show them You are here." He showed them all right, and the fire came down and licked up everything, including the water.

It is not always desirable to be on the mount all the time; and certainly, I do not enjoy being surrounded by the enemy; but I do want to stay in the place where I have to have God. To be in lineal descent and spiritual succession I have to live a little bit hazardously.

It never occurred to the apostles or to the apostolic Church that they could bring in a big shot and forget God. They followed Christ. They loved the Lord and the Lord added to the Church daily such as should be saved. They showed their spirituality by their attitude toward God, and we can prove ours only if we have a similar attitude toward God.

Attitude Toward the Holy Spirit

The next mark of identification is our *attitude toward the Holy Spirit*. A great indignity has been heaped upon the third person of the Trinity. Some have declared an end to His gifts, and it follows, therefore, an end to the Holy Spirit.

I believe in the gifts of the Spirit, and I believe they all ought to be in the church. I not only believe they all ought to be in the church, but I also believe they all are in the true church of Christ. However, there has been this great indignity heaped upon the Holy Spirit. Some say the gifts of the Spirit ceased with the death of the apostles. Why they fixed on that arbitrary time I do not know, because we do not know the date of the last apostle, and for that reason, we do not know when the Holy Spirit ceased to have any power among us.

So the Holy Spirit gets into the benediction and verse three of hymn number nine. Further than that, the Holy Spirit is not necessary to the church; we have arranged it so that He is not required. He has been displaced by what we call programming and by social activity.

The New Testament Church was born out of fire, and if "this" is going to be "that," then we are going to have to be born out of the same fire. Not all of the books we have or the creedal niceties we can quote will prove anything.

The Holy Spirit power is as necessary to the apostolic succession as breath is necessary to you. You have to breathe to live, and you need the Holy Spirit to live. If we do not have the Holy Spirit, if He is not here in power, we may be in creedal descent of the apostles but in creed only; we are not the children of the apostles.

The doctrine of the Holy Spirit has fallen into disrepute. Many people are worried about it, and in our schools they give three or four theories and tell you to take your choice. The man that is not convinced enough about the Holy Spirit to have only one theory ought to go out and plow corn; he ought not to be in the pulpit at all. If he has a half dozen possible theories that may be true, but he is altogether too broad and too charitable ever to insist on just one, then he ought to be somewhere else.

If the Holy Spirit ever comes on you, your fear will all go up and be replaced by certainty, and you will be able to teach the Word of God with prophetic certainty. We must have the same relation to the Holy Spirit that the apostolic Church had if we want to claim that we are in spiritual succession.

Attitude Toward the Flesh

The next mark of identity is our *attitude toward the flesh*. The New Testament Church repudiated the flesh. "Flesh" does not refer to your mortal body, for God has not anything against your mortal body. Your flesh is your personality, your ego.

The New Testament Church testified that they were baptized into Christ's death. When He arose, they arose; and when they arose, they arose in Him, and the old flesh was dead, and they were new creatures in Christ Jesus. That is what they taught. Paul taught that when believers were baptized, that is what happened. The old was gone, and they had new life in Christ Jesus the Lord.

We say that we are in spiritual succession from the apostles and the apostolic Church because we believe what they believed. However, is our attitude toward the flesh the same as theirs? Many churches incorporate the flesh right into their program and manage somehow to glorify the flesh and even write books to show that it should be there.

They take the flesh that God has condemned and nurse it back to life. They feed it and make it slick and smooth; educate it and call it by nice names. Then the church adopts it and elects it to the board and makes ushers and deacons out of it. Churches are organized around the flesh now and with the values and standards of the flesh. However, it is the flesh that the early Christians believed they left in the waters of baptism. It is that flesh the Early Church said died with Christ when He died on the cross.

I am not an old man sour on the world. I love everybody. It is not because I am older than I was 20 years ago; it is just plain

Bible truth. I believed it then, I believe it now; and I hope to believe it when the chariot comes for me that the people of God and the world have different standards. Flesh has no place in the kingdom of God at all. We ought to rule it out; we ought to, by the power of the Spirit and the power of the blood, get rid of the old man with his deeds. We must put it off as we would put off an old coat and put on the new man, which in Christ Jesus is renewed unto righteousness and true holiness.

Attitude Toward the World

Another mark of our identity with the apostolic Church is our *attitude toward the world.* The apostolic Church fled the world. Those early Christians were crucified to the world, and the world hated them. They remembered what Jesus said, "If the world hate you, ye know that it hated me before it hated you" (John 15:18). They heard the apostle John say, "Love not the world, neither the things that are in the world. If any man love the world, the love of the Father is not in him" (1 John 2:15).

We have a good deal of unpleasant things to say about the liberals because the liberals rule out certain passages of Scripture. I was reading a book the other day that explained which gospels were valid and what parts were written by nice people who did not know any better. I still believe that the Bible is God's Word, including 1 John 2:15, which is not a popular passage anymore; people do not want to hear it. We have adopted the world, conformed to it and identified ourselves with it all. Except of course the worst parts, like bank robbery and drug abuse; we do not commit them, but then the average sinner does not either.

We congratulate ourselves because we live as clean as the cultured people who attend opera; we live as decent as the atheist who does not believe in God and the scientist who believes that God is energy. We ought to be saved from that completely, but the truth is, we have sold out to the world.

Modern evangelicalism has surrendered to the world, excused it, explained it, adopted it and imitated it. More young preachers imitate men in the world with a good deal more energy than they imitate the holy saints of God. They are not interested in the saints and in imitating the saints of God, but rather they are interested in imitating the world and taking it in.

I might say that the church that has taken in the world has been taken in already. The world usually takes the church in before the church takes the world in. That church is not in succession from the apostles even if it has a creed drawn from the epistles of Paul, and even if it sticks to the doctrines of the faith. Christ is saying, "I know you are the seed of the apostles, but you are not of the children of the apostles." We have more liberal morals in evangelical circles than we have biblical.

Attitude Toward Worship

The last mark of identity with the apostolic church is our *identity of worship*. Jesus Christ our Lord located the kingdom of God within. God is within you, and some have told us that it means the kingdom was among you. It did not mean anything of the sort. It meant the kingdom of God lies inside your breast. Paul later said, "Christ in you, the hope of glory" (Col. 1:27). In addition, Jesus said, "God is a Spirit: and they that worship him must worship him in spirit and in truth" (John 4:24). We have an inward worship; the whole center and core of Christianity lies inside the heart.

We have externalized worship in our churches. Jesus put it in our heart and we have put it in side rooms. Jesus put it in our heart, but we have put it in the projection booth. The average Christian cannot practice his religion now any more than a Catholic priest can without his oil bottle and beads. If you cannot practice your worship with nothing in your hand but your Bible, you have not got victory. Nobody needs to claim succession from the apostolic church if he has to support his Christianity with a lot of gadgets, spending millions of dollars.

Most churches and pastors are addicted to gadgets and could not run their church without being more cluttered up with a small truckload of junk than you can climb up a moonbeam. We have fixed it that way, and it is taught in Bible college.

It used to be that a boy on one end of a log and William Tennent on the other end made a college. It used to be that one man of God surrounded by a little company of people made the Church. Not anymore, and yet we piously say that we are in lineal descent from the apostles. "We be not born of fornication; we have one Father, even God" (John 8:41). Jesus patiently said, "I know your creed is the same, but this did not Abraham."

We have to have an identity of worship with that apostolic Church. This worship is absent in the average church.

We have bushels of religious gatherings but only once in a great while is God in the midst. I would walk through mud up to my knees to get to a group where nobody was showing off, where only God was present. The Early Church prayed—talked to God. When they sang, they talked to God and sang about God. Today we have programming, that awful, hateful word "programming"; but God is absent.

The Early Church were worshipers; and when an unbeliever came in among them they said, "God is among them, of a truth." It was not the personality of the speaker; they might not have even had one. It was the presence of the Lord that made them fall down and worship. I will join anything, any group, when I can go in to and spend 10 minutes and come away relaxed and say, "I've been where God was." They were like that in apostolic times.

We say that we believe what the apostles believed, but I wonder if we are one with them in the succession of spiritual worship. I doubt it.

The True Church

There is a great danger that we shall assume too much and be absolutely convinced that we are the direct spiritual succession of the apostles, and piety will peter out with us. Remember, Israel had miracles in their history, but all the miracles of Israel did not keep them from the judgment of God. And the very people who were physical descendents of the miraculous work of God were scattered to the ends of the earth.

God wants us to be in spiritual succession with the apostles. He wants us to be in moral descent from the Early Church and to give the Holy Spirit the same place in our church that they gave Him in the Book of Acts. He wants us to make Jesus

Christ the central figure in our church—not say that we do, but actually do it. And if we do not, then we are only fooling ourselves. I do not want to be fooled by anybody, and I do not want to fool anybody.

I want to know whether I am in spiritual descent from the apostles or not; and if not, I want to do something about it. "If my people, which are called by my name, shall humble themselves, and pray, and seek my face, and turn from their wicked ways; then will I hear from heaven, and will forgive their sin, and will heal their land" (2 Chron. 7:14).

I want my little work to be solid gold the whole way through. I want it to be in my heart that I am in descent from the apostles—not as big as they were, but as real as they were and as spiritual as they were. I believe that is possible for any one of us.

I do not think there is a church in the United States but can have the same intensity of spiritual devotion that they had in the Book of Acts. If there is a church anywhere in the world that can have the same purity of life, intensity of worship and the same liberty in the Holy Spirit, and the same high moral level that we see in the Book of Acts and the epistles, then that church is in apostolic succession. If our churches do not have these marks of identification, then by no wild flight of the imagination can we dare to say that we are indeed in succession and in descent from the apostolic church. Physical descent is not sufficient, just as physical descent was not sufficient for Israel.

You must be what the apostles were and what the Early Church held as its standard, and then your people will tend to be like you. Then with joy in our hearts, we can know that we are descended from the apostles.

The Church's One Foundation
By Samuel J. Stone (1839-1900)

The Church's one foundation
Is Jesus Christ her Lord;
She is His new creation
By water and the word.
From heav'n He came and sought her
To be His holy bride;
With His own blood He bought her,
And for her life He died.

Elect from ev'ry nation,
Yet one o'er all the earth,
Her charter of salvation
One Lord, one faith, one birth;
One holy name she blesses;
Partakes one holy food,
And to one hope she presses,
With ev'ry grace endued.

Yet she on earth hath union
With God the three in one,
And mystic sweet communion
With those whose rest is won;
O happy ones and holy!
Lord, give us grace that we,
Like them, the meek and lowly,
On high may dwell with Thee.

'Mid toil and tribulation
And tumult of her war,
She waits the consummation
Of peace forevermore;
Till with the vision glorious
Her longing eyes are blest,
And the great Church victorious,
Shall be the Church at rest.

Though with a scornful wonder
Men see her sore oppressed,
By schisms rent asunder,
By heresies distressed:
Yet saints their watch are keeping,
Their cry goes up, "how long?"
And soon the night of weeping
Shall be the morn of song.

4

THE OMINOUS ECUMENICAL MOVEMENT

And all that believed were together,
and had all things common.

ACTS 2:44

One of the dearest doctrines in the Scriptures, in my opinion, is the unity of the church of Christ, not only one with each other, but also one with Christ.

There is a movement on, and has been for some time, to bring all the Church into one organization. The word "ecumenical" simply means universal, all over the earth. That is all it means, but it has been adapted to mean that all over the earth, where there are Christians, they are in one organization. It does not mean the whole Church. If there is an ecumenical council, it does not mean that all the churches are there, but it does mean that all are represented or that the representatives of the whole Church are there.

Then there are those—though they would not say this was their reason—who just want to get together with all like-minded Christians, and that is a fine. There have been quite a number of mergers in recent times, and some of them have been right. They are all believers, they all get together, and instead of having two heads and two headquarters and two official magazines, they only have one. That is always to be desired.

Then we have a movement among the Protestants with certain aims. One of the aims I do not believe in at all, because I think it has already been fulfilled. Our Lord, when He prayed, "That they all may be one; as thou, Father, art in me, and I in thee, that they also may be one in us: that the world may believe that thou hast sent me" (John 17:21), wanted His church to be one, and He prayed in that direction. Now the ecumenical movement is saying, "You need to join our organization for the unification of believers so that the prayer of Jesus would be fulfilled that 'all may be one.'"

Some believe that Christians ought to get together and fulfill the prayer of Christ, even if they have to sacrifice truth. It started in Amsterdam in 1948, during the great world movement called the World Council of Churches. I do not make it a practice to preach against things. I am 99 percent for things and 1 percent against. This happens to be one of the things I am against. The Anglicans, the Eastern Orthodox, the Protestants and the old Catholics got together. Then into the World Council of Churches have come denominations or at least parts of denominations until it is a vast, sprawling octopus all over the world.

Christendom Is Not the Church

I would like to say that if it takes Jesus Christ 1,900 years to get His prayer answered for the unity of His church, and if all down the centuries this has not been answered, and the Church has yet to become unified, then my faith in the Lord would suffer a staggering blow. The simple fact is that the prayer of Jesus was answered dramatically in the fiery outpouring at Pentecost when all believers were baptized by the Holy Spirit into one Body.

One thing we ought to remember is that the unity of the Christian church in the Spirit is one thing, but the union of all Christian groups is quite another thing altogether. We ought to remember the doctrine of apostasy found in the Scriptures. "For the time will come when they will not endure sound doctrine; but after their own lusts shall they heap to themselves teachers, having itching ears; and they shall turn away their ears from the truth, and shall be turned unto fables" (2 Tim. 4:3-4).

There is much else there where it said that a time would come when men would be lovers of their own selves and having the form of godliness but denying the power thereof; and he said from such to turn away.

There is a fundamental difference between Christendom and the Church. What the present ecumenical push is trying to do is solidify Christendom—all who are on the Christian side of things in any way—and bring them together in one vast body. That is Christendom. But there is in the Scriptures a great difference between Christendom and the Church. The Bible teaches that Christendom shall be apostate and shall give up their faith and shall wallow in her own self-righteousness and deny the power of God and shall be totally unprepared for the coming of the Lord Jesus Christ. When the Son of man cometh, will He find faith in the earth? That is Christendom. But the Church is another thing.

What I desire is the beautiful church of Christ that we read about in Ephesians:

One Lord, one faith, one baptism, One God and Father of all, who is above all, and through all, and in you all. But unto every one of us is given grace according to the measure of the gift of Christ. Wherefore he saith, when he ascended up on high, he led captivity captive, and gave gifts unto men. (Now that he ascended, what is it but that he also descended first into the lower parts of the earth? He that descended is the same also that ascended up far above all heavens, that he might fill all things.) And he gave some, apostles; and some, prophets; and some, evangelists; and some, pastors and teachers; for the perfecting of the saints, for the work of the ministry, for the edifying of the body of Christ: till we all come in the unity of the faith, and of the knowledge of the Son of God, unto a perfect man, unto the measure of the stature of the fulness of Christ (Eph. 4:5-13).

The perfecting of this unity takes place when anyone is baptized by the Spirit into the Body of Christ. The perfecting of that Body, until the whole beautiful Church is brought into the presence of Christ, is the business of the Holy Ghost through the Scriptures, and through pastors and teachers and prayer warriors on the earth. In the meantime, there is a great body called Christendom made up of Christians of every stripe, color and kind throughout the whole world. This is not included here, and the Holy Spirit never intended it to be here.

Guarding the Church Against Christendom

What can we do to guard ourselves from this kind of thing in the Church? The primary thing we need to keep in mind is to join nothing that questions the truth of the Bible. Any movement, any church or group anywhere that questions the truth of the Bible is one that you, as a believer, cannot afford to associate with. If this group allows any place for all the superstition that goes along with holy bones and holy water and the Mother of God and all mankind, the sane thing is to quietly walk out.

I have never left anything and never split anything. So I am neither a lint picker nor a witch hunter. And I am not compelling every man to say *"Shibboleth"* (see Judg. 12) in the same tone of voice I do. If he has an Irish accent and says *Shibboleth* some other way, let him say it. If he loves the Lord, he is my brother. But if he is a smooth talker and tells me it is ridiculous to believe that God ever inspired the Scriptures, then I cannot have fellowship with him.

The seventeenth chapter of Revelation tells about that great mystery the Babylonian, the great mother of harlots, the abomination of the earth. This harlot has children. She not only is a harlot but she is the mother of other harlots, and these harlots are nothing else than apostate churches claiming the name of the Lord but not living the truth of the Lord.

I am not a good enough prophet to know what direction things are going to take. But I do know that I hear strange things in evangelical circles these days. I hear people rethinking things. We are rethinking inspiration; we are rethinking the deity of Christ; we are rethinking sin; we are rethinking morals and trying to equate it with what they call morays, or habits and customs, of certain cultures. We have gone to anthropology and have learned that what is a sin in one country is not necessarily so in another and, therefore, we Christians have to accept whatever is there. We are rethinking things. We are even rethinking whether God created the heavens and the earth, and man after His own image.

The evangelicals are now rethinking things that evangelicals took for granted a generation ago. So I do not know what direction we are going to go from here. But I believe we ought to obey the Word of God and withdraw from all that deny it in any fashion.

I can tell you this: While I live, there will be one free Protestant. I know not what others may do, said the old politician, but as for me "give me liberty or give me death." And as for me, I know not what others may do. But while I live, there will be one free Protestant. I may be in jail, but I will be free. A man who believes in God through Jesus Christ the Lord knows where he is and is not going to be brainwashed by soft talk. That is a free Protestant, even if he is in chains.

We are asked to surrender to the movement that would unite us all together and make a great, vast, sprawling super-church out of all Christians. Some drink, some dance, some live wickedly, some are mad about money, some never go to church except once a year on one of the holidays. Some doubt the Word of God, and some deny it, and some will laugh at it. Some gamble and some play the horses; some are dirty minded and tell dirty jokes, and yet they belong to the different churches. And they want me to join that mess. To join it would be to surrender; and to surrender would be to perish.

I cannot have much influence on the evangelical church. But I should like to say to the evangelical church that there is a little limerick by Cosmo Monkhouse (1840-1901) they ought to remember:

There was a young lady of Niger
Who smiled as she rode on a Tiger;
They came back from the ride
With the lady inside,
And the smile on the face of the Tiger.

Whether this makes me popular or unpopular, I care not at all. But there is a difference between the ecumenical movement, which would unify in one great super organization all people who say they are Christians, and the true Church, which is a living organism born of the Spirit, washed in the blood of Christ and joined to the Body of Christ by a mysterious operation of the Holy Ghost called regeneration.

I want you in the meantime to know that I am for the Church, but I am not for the great world superchurch. I am for the Church, which Jesus Christ purchased with His blood.

Drawn Together by the Holy Spirit

Why was the Early Church gathered together, this beautiful crowd of believers? They were together because of a variety of reasons. They were pressed together by antagonisms from the outside and thrown together by the magnetism from the inside.

They were a body of Christians living clean and right. Because they dared to take their stand and to be counted on the issues that matter, they were likely to get pushed together and pressed together by external antagonisms. But that was not enough. They must be drawn together by internal magnetism. That is, they (and we) must be drawn together by the Holy Spirit.

I love the people of God. I am a nervous man, and sometimes I cannot spend a lot of time with people. The pressure of hard work keeps me rather jumpy, and so I do not say that I always like to sit down and talk five hours with everybody, but I love the Lord's people. I love the old weary women; I love the bright-eyed young fellow just converted. I love God's people. If they are in Christ, I love them, and that magnetism would bring me to the church of Christ. Do not imagine that I have not down the years said, "Well I'm going to quit preaching." But as David said, "My heart was hot within me, while I was musing the fire burned: then spake I with my tongue," (Ps. 39:3), and I went back to preaching again.

Sheep are not solitary creatures. They work together, live together, feed together and lie down together in the green pastures beside the soft waters. The only time a sheep goes off by itself is when he is lost or sick. A sick sheep does not go with the flock; and when I find a Christian who is such an individualist that he never goes to church, he is a sick Christian. So if you are a healthy sheep, you will go where the flock is. If you wonder where the Shepherd is, I would like to tell you: He is where the flock is.

If any of you wonder where the flock is, I would like to tell you that it is where the Shepherd is. So the Shepherd and the flock always stay together, and I, for my part, have neither the courage nor the disposition to go off by myself and try to live my Christian life all alone. I need others; I need the other sheep that are of the fold and the other sheep that are not of this fold but are coming into the fold.

The Communion of the Saints

A Christian does not dwell alone, and Christians should stay together for the mutual help they can be to each other. If you think that you do not need the Church, it is proof that you do need the Church. If you did not need the Church, you would probably think you did. It is the same as when a man says he is not sick but it is obvious that he is. He is worse off than the man who knows he is sick. For the man who is sick and does not know he is sick and will not admit it is not going to go anywhere for help.

There is such a thing as a communion of saints and a cultivation of eternal friendships. You can say good-bye to people here at their graveside and meet them again with a warm, immortal handshake at the right hand of God. You can know them, recognize them and know them for who they are and were. So we need each other.

The communion of saints—I do not want to make too much of it. I do not want to make too much of anything unless it is possible to make too much of Christ. I do not want to preach every time about the communion of saints, nevertheless, I believe in the communion of saints. I believe in the communion of the saints of God on the earth and the communion of the saints of God who have gone from the earth. You say, "Then you believe in spirit tapping and communicating with somebody that is gone." I did not say communicate, I said commune. There is a difference. I do not believe it is possible to communicate with the saints in heaven, but I think it is possible to have communion with them.

Suppose a man and a young woman were in love and the man had to leave her and go away to another province somewhere, another state. He said, "Listen, we will be a long, long way apart, but I'll tell you what you do."

And he looked at his calendar and said, "At a certain night at a certain hour the moon will be full, and it will be in a certain position at a certain time in the evening of a certain night. Now I can't come to you, but you go out on the lawn and you look at the moon; and I'll go out on the lawn and I'll look at the moon; and I'll be looking at what you're looking at, and we'll be seeing the same thing, and we'll be thinking about each other."

That may be a little romantic, but there is something to it. We look at Jesus and they look at Jesus, and though they are over yonder and we are here, we are the church militant and they are the church triumphant, but we meet in the same Person. We do not communicate with each other, just as the young man and the young woman do not yahoo across the meadow to each other because they are too far apart. I believe it is entirely possible to have the communion of saints, which is a unity of appreciation, a unity of love, a unity of worship, a unity of devotion, and more than that, a union in the Holy Spirit, which makes all the people of God one around the world.

I do not know whether I will take my sense of humor to heaven or not. I do not go in much for these articles proving that God has a sense of humor. But I think I may keep mine in the world to come, and I think I am going to laugh, at least with a certain amount of celestial dignity, when I see the astonished look on the face of some people who did not think I was going to get there.

"Oh," they will exclaim in disbelief, "you didn't belong to our denomination at all."

"No, I didn't belong to your denomination, but I got here."

The look of astonishment is going to please me. I think I am going to laugh, because I believe that all the people of God are going to make it through without any effort at all, through the blood of the everlasting covenant. There is the communion, so therefore I want to commune with the people of God.

There is always safety near the Shepherd. It can be suicide for a sheep to stray from the Shepherd; so if you stay close by the Shepherd, you will not only be near the Shepherd but you also will be near to each other. Isn't that reasonable? You crowd in to the Shepherd; you get nearer to each other.

I grieve that we have so little manifestation of the Shepherd's presence in our churches. We talk about His being here, but we do not sense that He is here. We do not have the feeling that He is here. Do not talk down feeling, for it's part of our human constitution; and when He walks into the presence of His people consciously, they cannot help but feel it.

I think that the most wonderful thing would be to each become so Christ-conscious and so Church-loving that we would clean up our lives and purify our hearts and wash our hands and forgive our enemies and love them too. Then we would focus on Him and learn to live and pray and preach and give and worship in the very conscious presence of the Son of God's love. I think this would be the most beautiful thing in the whole wide world.

I do not mind telling you that if I knew there was any place on the earth where a company of believers enjoyed this as intensely and wonderfully as they should, I think I would try to find them and, if they would have me, spend the rest of my days with them. That is a sweet company when the Lord is in the midst of it.

The King of Love My Shepherd Is
By Henry W. Baker (1821-1877)

The King of love my Shepherd is,
Whose goodness faileth never;
I nothing lack if I am His
And He is mine forever.

Where streams of living water flow
My ransomed soul He leadeth,
And, where the verdant pastures grow,
With food celestial feedeth.

Perverse and foolish oft I strayed,
But yet in love He sought me,
And on His shoulder gently laid,
And home rejoicing brought me.

In death's dark vale I fear no ill
With Thee, dear Lord beside me;
Thy rod and staff my comfort still,
Thy cross before to guide me.

And so through all the length of days
Thy goodness faileth never;
Good Shepherd, may I sing Thy praise
Within Thy house forever.

5

THE DAUNTING SPIRIT OF THE PHARISEES

And it came to pass, as he went into the house of one of the chief
Pharisees to eat bread on the sabbath day, that they watched him.
And, behold, there was a certain man before him which had the dropsy.
And Jesus answering spake unto the lawyers and Pharisees, saying,
Is it lawful to heal on the sabbath day? And they held their peace.
And he took him, and healed him, and let him go; and answered them,
saying, which of you shall have an ass or an ox fallen into a pit, and
will not straightway pull him out on the sabbath day? And they
could not answer him again to these things.

LUKE 14:1-6

We have in this brief passage a real-life drama of redemption
and, as in the other scenes, the self-righteous religionist, the
poor needy man and the Lord of glory. The circumstances are
about the same: the man who is marked with death.

Luke, who wrote this story, was a physician trained in the
finest schools of his day; and when Luke says a man had a disease, he names the disease. This man had a disease called dropsy,
marked with death. And here alongside, calloused to their knees,

were the self-righteous text quoters who cared not for him and could not help him.

Here is the heaviest thought to bear, to see the orthodox people of their day who could quote you Scripture, and they were right. They were not cultists, they were not fanatics, they were not wild, unorganized or unauthorized religious leaders. They sat in Moses' seat; they taught the Scriptures; they were orthodox; they could show you books proving they were right. But, they were hard-hearted and arrogant. Can it be so that a man can be orthodox—sound in his creed and loyal to his denomination, loyal to the church of his fathers—and still be blind, cruel, bigoted and wicked?

In contrast to these Pharisees in the story is the strong Son of God present and tolerant toward their blindness and cruelty. Not that He in any wise condoned them; He would die for them but never compromise with them. But He was tolerant, nevertheless, and eager to help the man marked with death—this man who had the swelling disease, the disease refusing to allow the body to discharge its excess liquid contents and piled it into the cells until the body swells, and finally the poor heart cannot take it, and he dies.

In the story of the leper, we get an accurate picture of the conflict between Jesus and the religious leaders of His day. Could it be that we, as we look out upon the world and have tried to identify ourselves and our times, have placed the battle where the battle is not? Could it be that we have located the conflict where it is not? Could it be that we have looked to the gamblers and horse racers as the enemy, and certainly, they are no friends of God? Could it be we have looked at peddlers and the marijuana pushers and said, "There is the enemy"? We have looked at the much-abused American businessman with his carelessness toward heaven and his absorption with earth and said, "Secularism is the enemy." Could it be that we see the battle where the battle is not and the conflict where God does not find it? Could it be that the conflict is not with a harlot, a gambler and the worldly businessman, but with the religionists? And could it be that the trouble with the world is the kind of religion that we have?

I believe the clash with Jesus, in this story, could not be with the sinner, for He came to die for sinners. The conflict was with a group that had a correct and proper understanding; they could look at need and not care, behold men and not feel a tremor of sympathy. They spoke of their respectability, congratulated themselves once a day on their creedal correctness, and yet, had no heart for the poor, love for the harlot and no sympathy for the ignorant. That is a description of the religionists, not only of Jesus' time, but of ours as well.

In this story, we have confusion and opposition to goodness. It seems the only strong hand was the one that was soon to be pierced by a nail, and the only pure heart was one that was soon to beat itself out and stop on a cross. And the only clear head was the one that was soon to bow in death, and the only significant voice was the one that would soon be silent in death.

If man had written the Gospels—say William Shakespeare or Eugene O'Neill—the story of the gospel would have been drastically different. They would have placed the prince in halls and palaces and had him walking among the great. They would have had him surrounded by the important and significant of the time. Potentates and kings would have been His companions. But how sweetly common was the real God-man; though He had inhabited all eternity, He had come down and was subject to the rising and the setting of the sun.

Here was the difference between the Pharisees and Christ. To Christ, sin was not contagious. Sin was a disease of the soul, and Jesus knew a pure heart needed no protection. The Pharisee thought sin was contagious, and infectious by contact, and so they kept from their houses these common people—these harlots from the red light areas, the Publicans and tax gatherers, the common masses that cross the streets of the city. They ruled them all out. But they—the Pharisees—were the elite, the elect, the religious, the friends of God, the chosen ones. Or so they thought.

You cannot keep religion pure by keeping it insular and away from the crowds. The poor of our day, the poor church of the century, has had to seal up its pitiful little purity and take its tiny might of godliness to a monastery and cut it off from the market place to keep it pure. The poor, pitiful manliness had to be clothed in black robes and hide in a cave to keep pure.

Even in Protestant circles we have to clothe the clergy with a robe so he will not lose his godliness on his way to the pulpit. And some of the stricter sects have shut themselves off completely from the world.

In Indiana, Ohio and Pennsylvania, the Amish, a religious sect, will not ride an automobile; they drive buggies. I guess there is less likelihood of springing a moral leak and losing your spirituality if you are behind a horse than if you ride fast behind a wheel. What nonsense.

The fountain of spirituality flows outward. You cannot contaminate a fountain, because the fountain within him shall flow out. Any contagion or infection that comes from the outside is automatically rendered new by the outflow. If it came from the world, it could bring its pollution with it; but because it is the outflow from within him, it is not affected by the world.

The religionists watched and suspected this radical Jesus. With all their disputing minds they watched Him.

Remember, Christ is not now on trial. Then He stood before their approval. Now God has raised Him to His own right hand, and the message now is an offer of life. The Son of God is no longer before the watchful judges of earth since the Holy Spirit has come and has confirmed His deity, declaring Him to be the Son of God with power by the resurrection from the dead. Jesus stood and was watched by the religionists of His day; but He has risen beyond their power and has been declared the Son of God with power by the resurrection from the dead.

The evil Pharisees had the power to instantly arrest; and if they had hitched up the side one inch, like a pack of hungry wolves, they would have had Him in prison in one hour's time. However, He outmatched them all. He stood in their midst, and by their silence they admitted that in Him they found no guilt.

Then He turned on them and said, "I want to ask you theologians, is it legal to do good on the Sabbath day?" That question had in it a whole world of accusation. He was saying by that question, "I know that you are Pharisees, I know you're strict with the law. I know you bring your children to the temple when they're eight days old to circumcise them and return when they are 12 to confirm them. I know what you do to them and I know what you are. I know you are religious, I know your cold, hard hearts. You care nothing for the blind and the poor that hobble by."

Then, to rub in the salt into the trembling, jerking religionist, he said, "Which of you shall have an ass or an ox fallen into a pit, and will not straightway pull him out on the sabbath day?" (Luke 14:5). They knew they would. They had so manipulated the law to permit them to save money on the Sabbath day, but their hearts could not rise to believe that you could save a human life. He knew that; He pressed it home on them, and they looked at each other until they could not bear the sight and looked down and were still.

T. DeWitt Talmage (1832-1902) told this story. A Universalist went into a certain neighborhood, intending to start a Universalist church. So he looked around and inquired if any Universalist lived in that neighborhood, and they said, "Yes, there was one Universalist."

The minister visited this man and told him that he was trying to establish a church of that denomination in the area, and would he support it?

The man said, "I'm a Universalist all right, but I'm a little different kind of Universalist from what you are. You believe in the universal salvation of everybody. But I've been out in the world a lot; I've lived a while, and I have been betrayed and lied to and cheated and abused and injured until I have come to believe in the universal damnation of all men."

I fear the respectable, godly, self-contained people who have money, who dress well, have good educations, speak good English and read good books but have no heart for the flow of humanity that flows everywhere. They care not for the poor and the distressed. I am afraid of aloof godliness—you lovely women who pay no attention to the very women that need you. You respectable men with your money, you hold yourself aloof from a man that needs you the worst.

Jesus healed the man marked with death and let him go. I do not know what He did to him. But He walked over to the man with eyes bulging, cells filled with water, legs heavy and swollen. If the man could stand at all, it was only with great effort. Perhaps he could no longer stand. He was just a great form lying there. They knew no way to help the man, but Christ took him.

Christ took pity on the sheep without a shepherd. He took Elisha from the plow. He took Peter from fishing, Saul from the Supreme Court, Augustine from the evil religion. He took John Bunyan, John Newton, Charles Finney and Billy Sunday. He took them and He has a way of doing that.

People often come up to me and ask, "Mr. Tozer, I've heard you talk, I've read your books; now tell us how it's done." That very fact rules them out.

There is a point where no preacher can help you, and a personal worker is useless. There is a place where the soul sees a black abyss, and God leaps into the black abyss.

Whoever will confine this to mere physical healing is a million miles off. Christ does heal physically sometimes, and He will, at death, give deliverance. He gave the man who was close to death the help he needed. That is conversion. I do not know how He does it. I only know that He does it, and I can only point and say, "He is the one to go to." After that, you are on your own, and He will take you.

There is a prevalent position I have heard of recently that says: "Religion is a change of prison, that is all." You are in prison, and then you become religious and change the worldly prison for religious prison. It is just a change of prisons. If anybody says, "I was in a world prison and now I'm in Christ's prison," then shame on you. Shake your hand and see if there is any manacle on it. Kick your foot a bit and see if there is any ball and chain there. Look up and see if you see any steel bars. Look down and see if you see flagstone. Walk out and nobody will challenge you and say, "Who goes there?" You are free as a bird that swings and sings in yonder blue heaven.

The best answer to the charge that religion is a change of prison is to ask the people who know God whether they are that way or not. The only freedom I have ever known in all my years of life is the freedom Jesus Christ gives me. And if I would give Him up and turn away from it all, I would be the victim of my luck and my pride, my temper and my sulky disposition, my hatefulness and my fear. I would be surrounded by bars that I could not saw my way through in a thousand years. But when He took me, He also said, "Now, go."

The Christian is the freest man in the world. He is free to be good and generous; free to be free; free from fear and free from revenge. He is free.

The meaning of the word "redemption" is threefold. It means to buy in the market, to buy out of the market and to set free. Jesus bought the man with His own blood, because later He was to die for him. He took him out of the market; he was no longer for sale. There was no price tag saying he was marked down or soiled. There was no tag saying, "Sale today." There is no tag on you, no price tag. You had a price tag on you once that nobody could pay.

The Seraphims did not have fire enough and the cherubims did not have purity enough. The angels and principalities and watchers and holy ones did not have gold or silver enough. You were not redeemed with corruptible things but by the blood of the Lamb of God who without spot or wrinkle went out to die. That was the price. Nobody could pay it, but He paid it. He could take this man, convert him and let him go because He paid the price for him, potentially and actually.

Have you been captured by the Lord Jesus Christ? Have you been converted and set free? If not, then you may be the victim. Just a church member—a formal church member surrounded by those who make you feel all right when you are not all right.

Do not ask me to give you the trick; there is no trick in it. You go to Jesus Christ as you are—weary, worn and sad. You will find in Him a resting place and He will make you glad. You come to Jesus with blindness and He makes you see. Come with your deafness and He makes you hear. Come in your bondage and He sets you free.

Thank God for the Strong Man who walked among them. Those textualists, those Pharisees, would have lugged that great swollen body out and lowered it down in a hole and said some Hebrew words, wiped their hands clean and walked away and said, "That's done." That is all they had; they were the religious leaders of their day, but all they had to offer was a grave. But Jesus Christ pushed the grave years into the future and gave the man a long, happy life to live. He was able to live in the sweet knowledge that the Messiah had come and delivered him.

Shall it be a religion or shall it be Christ? Shall it be church-ianity or shall it be Jesus Christ? Shall it be pride or shall it be humility in Jesus Christ? Humble yourselves therefore unto the mighty hand of God. Jesus will not walk with the proud and the scornful; so humble yourself to walk with God.

O Love, How Deep

Latin, Fifteenth Century
Translated by Benjamin Webb (1819-1885)

O love, how deep, how broad, how high,
it fills the heart with ecstasy,
that God, the Son of God, should take
our mortal form for mortals' sake!

He sent no angel to our race
of higher or of lower place,
but wore the robe of human frame
Himself, and to this lost world came.

For us baptized, for us he bore
his holy fast and hungered sore,
for us temptation sharp he knew;
for us the tempter overthrew.

For us he prayed; for us he taught;
for us his daily works he wrought;
by words and signs and actions thus
still seeking not himself, but us.

For us to wicked men betrayed,
scourged, mocked, in purple robe arrayed,
he bore the shameful cross and death,
for us at length gave up his breath.

For us he rose from death again;
for us he went on high to reign;
for us he sent his Spirit here
to guide, to strengthen and to cheer.

To him whose boundless love has won
salvation for us through his Son,
to God the Father, glory be
both now and through eternity.

6

BEWARE OF THE RELIGIOUS WORD GAME

*For our gospel came not unto you in word only, but also in power,
and in the Holy Ghost, and in much assurance; as ye know what
manner of men we were among you for your sake.*

1 THESSALONIANS 1:5

*Therefore if any man be in Christ, he is a new creature: old things are
passed away; behold, all things are become new.*

2 CORINTHIANS 5:17

*And unto the angel of the church in Sardis write; These things saith he
that hath the seven Spirits of God, and the seven stars; I know thy
works, that thou hast a name that thou livest, and art dead.*

REVELATION 3:1

The first text (1 Thess. 1:5) says that the gospel may come in one
of two ways. It may come in word only, which is empty, or it may
come in power, which is with moral effectiveness. Paul knew
that the gospel message had come to the Thessalonians effec-
tively, in moral power, and he gave as his reason that they had

much assurance and became followers of Christ, having received the Word in much affliction. Nothing could turn them back. They had a strange and supernatural joy, which Paul labeled the joy of the Holy Ghost; and they went on not only to be followers but examples to the other churches, and from them sounded out the Word of the Lord. They became a missionary church.

If it is true that that is what happens when the Word comes in power—and the text opens the doors to the belief that the Word can come nominally and without power—then exactly the opposite would be true. Without Holy Spirit power, they would become Christians by some decision, but without much assurance, and would not be followers of the Lord, except in name. When affliction came, they would not take it very well, and they would not have very much joy; they would have to work it up— it would not stay long. And they would not be very good examples; they would be lukewarm when it came to the missionary zeal. Now that is a fair explanation here, and it lies in this Thessalonian verse.

The second text (2 Cor. 5:17) says that the effect of the gospel, in addition to what Paul said in Thessalonians, when received in power, regenerates a man's nature. "Generate" means to create, and "regenerate" means to create again. That is what the Word does when it is received in power; the old things of the first generation, that is, the first creation, pass away, and everything becomes new. A set of new things takes the place of the old that was set aside when the Holy Ghost regenerated the heart to believe in the gospel.

The third text (Rev. 3:1) says there are those who have heard the gospel and are called Christians, but they are Christians in name only. That is what "nominal" means. They have not been changed fundamentally and are still old; they are still dead.

The reason God has to regenerate us is because sin came, and we died, and He has to do this life-giving job a second time in order that we might live. But there are some who have only changed in name. They have not been changed fundamentally at all. They still belong to the old life, and the Holy Spirit says they have a name to live, but actually they are dead.

This is a brief exegesis of these three great verses. I want you to see what it means to have the gospel come in word, and then what it means to have the gospel come in power. Then let's talk about the danger that it shall be only in word and not in power, and what we should do about it.

Nominal Christianity

Some believe the gospel but have it in word only. Our Lord Jesus taught this in Israel; He said, "Woe unto you, scribes and Pharisees, hypocrites! For ye are like unto whited sepulchres, which indeed appear beautiful outward, but are within full of dead men's bones, and of all uncleanness. Even so ye also outwardly appear righteous unto men, but within ye are full of hypocrisy and iniquity" (Matt. 23:27-28).

They looked at each other, tugged at their long beards and determined that as soon as possible, without a mob scene resulting, they would kill Jesus. Finally, they did kill Him, but God raised Him from the dead the third day and set Him at His own right hand. They thought they were murdering a man, but God was offering a sacrifice. That is the difference. That is the irony of fighting against the Lord Jesus Christ.

As a consequence of being a nominal Christian, in name only, there is a tendency to use words in a wrong way, to engage in religious word games. In too many places today, the Christian religion has simply been reduced to a word game.

Some say, "I know that very well, because I used to belong to the thus-and-thus denomination. I know that was true then, they were as dead as could be. The pastor did not believe in the virgin birth." Somebody else says, "I used to go to a church where they did not believe that Moses wrote the Pentateuch. They were scoundrels, they were liberals."

But the Holy Spirit is not talking about liberals or people who deny the truth of Scripture. He is talking about people who admit the truth of the Scripture and receive the gospel as a fact and do not deny it, but support it, follow it and would kick a pastor out if he did not preach it. But it has only reached them in words, because their religion is simply a word game.

Playing the Word Game

A game is something you do by creating a problem and then having fun solving it. I know a little about baseball, so I will use that for illustration. Baseball creates a problem and spends millions of dollars solving a problem that did not exist until they created it.

Abner Doubleday (1819-1893) is the one credited with inventing the game we now call baseball. He said, "I'll tell you what we'll do, we'll create a problem and then solve it. We'll put one man out here with a ball and put another man 60 feet away from him to catch the ball when thrown to him. Now the problem is for this man with the ball to throw it so the other man catches it, but in the meantime, in order to make it tough for this man to get the ball through to the other man, we are going to put a fellow in there with a stick. This man with the stick will stand there and try to keep that ball from getting to that other man's mitt. Now that problem is what we will work on. One fellow out here will be called the pitcher and will wind up and gyrate and throw the ball to the other man, who will catch it. Then, this fellow with the stick, he's the devil in between and he will try to keep the catcher from catching it."

And so the game of baseball was created. Games work that way. They have a problem, but the problem never existed before. There was polio, cancer, war and starvation, but they had to create a problem, and then put the healthiest men in the world to play at it.

This fellow throws the ball, and the fellow with the stick hauls off and swings the stick. And if he connects with the ball, the problem is solved in his favor. He is having fun. They hear the sound of the ball on wood and say, "I think it sounds like a homer." However, there are eight other men determined that he is not going to have that solution. They are going to have it, so they are the shortstop—three basemen and the three outfielders—they are all ready to catch that ball; and if anybody can get that ball before it hits the ground, the fellow with the stick is out.

We spend millions of dollars solving that problem hundreds of times on a sunny afternoon. That is a game and some people like games.

One thing about a game is that nobody is any better or worse for whatever happens. If the man with the stick wins, he's not any better off, he just goes home; and if his wife doesn't like him before, she still doesn't like him. And if he is in debt, he is still in debt; and if he has a disease, he still has a disease; and no matter what, he is still no better off, and the other fellow is no worse off.

Even in the Olympics, athletes compete with each other but it is all games, and when it is all over, they go home. Nobody is any better off or worse off because they created their problems before the athletes were sent over here to solve them.

When the Canadians and the Americans were fighting Hitler, it mattered who won, for it was a difference between slavery and living on your knees. It was the difference between playing a game and fighting a war.

In religion, the temptation is to take it as a word game. Instead of a baseball or a football, we have other gadgets that we throw around, like words. We write books, buy books, proofread books and sweat over books. We edit magazines. We buy magazines. We subscribe. We write songs. We sing songs. We make prayers. We say prayers. We preach sermons. We hear sermons.

All of this requires, of course, a vast amount of activity, and a tremendous amount of money, and a great deal of perspiration, and a lot of inconvenience, and a good deal of money. Yet a great number of people simply play the game of religious words. It makes no difference. The giveaway is that the religious word game does not change anybody fundamentally; they are not much different from what they were before.

A certain university sponsored a survey. They took 100 men who were devout churchmen and investigated their ethical standards in their business. Then they took a hundred men who never went to church and investigated their ethics to see how they ran their business."

After some time, and after spending a lot of money and doing a lot of investigating, they said, "By and large there isn't any difference between the ethical business standards of the religious churchman and the nonreligious man who never enters the church door."

We are just human beings, wherever we live and whatever our nationality. If it is true in one place, it is likely to be true in another. So what are these 100 men doing that have been investigated? They are just playing a word game. They go to church and maybe they are ushers, and down the aisle they go, looking dignified with a boutonniere in their lapels. Or they are preachers who stand up, take a text, breathe through their nose heavily, and preach the Word, and people say, "Wasn't that a great sermon." They shake his hand and say, "I was blessed," and go out. The next morning their business ethics have not been changed a bit. The pastor simply has had fun playing a word game.

We set up a problem and solve it. We throw a ball and somebody else with a stick hits it; and when it's all over, we say, "Boy, our church is growing, and we're known in the city. We're a great church, aren't we. Let's see what we can do to make the thing look better."

I want nothing to do with this religious word game. I want nobody fooling me with unreality. I do not want anybody coming and fawning over me if he does not mean it. I do not want anybody to lie to me in the name of etiquette or ask me for a dime to support something I do not believe in. I do not want anybody to ask me to believe in a religion that I have to take on the basis of somebody's authority. If Jesus Christ cannot change me; if my Christianity is not real; if the problem I face is not a real problem; if it does not mean heaven, hell, death and the grave; then I do not want to be wasting my time with it at all. I would rather take a walk and listen to the birds sing than listen to any man preach who tries to smooth me down or to put up a problem that does not exist and play with it. That is what is going on all the time.

The giveaway of this religious word game is that a person says he is fundamentally different, but the same old principles motivate the life. A man comes, says he is a Christian and wants to join the church. But his natural appetites are just the same, only refined a little bit, that is all. His egotism has not been destroyed, only less gross than it was before. It is possible for an egotist to get a college education and be a refined egotist, skillful at hiding the fact that he is an egotist. He can refine that still more by being converted. And the Word of the Lord will come to him but it will not come to him in power. All it does is refine his egotism.

Then there is the matter of selfishness. He is exactly the same selfish fellow he was before, only he has sanitized his selfishness a little bit now. And he loves games just as he always did, he just rubs his hands to see the money come in, only now he gives a little of it to the Lord and takes it off his income tax and feels that he is a saint. But all he has accomplished is what any sinner might do.

The trouble is, the roots of the life have not changed, which is why we are half-dead. That is why we are where we are—the roots of the life have not been changed. We are growing in the same old root as we were before when we were a religious man carrying a hymnbook or a Bible under our arm. That is why Christians are so largely ineffective.

The devil means what he is saying, and he is not fooling—Christians often are, but the devil never. Christians play word games, but the devil is not playing. When the gospel comes in power, we are not playing any more; it is real. Do not imagine for a minute that you can get away with this word game inside the church of Christ. God will not accept any tossing things around or playing with words or songs or sermons or books.

What happens to a man when he is really born anew? We use that phrase "born again" in evangelical circles. We have used it until it does not have any more meaning left. It is worn as thin as an old 1914 dime, but it is still in the Bible. You still have to be born again. That is, you have to be regenerated, made a new creature. Those are the same words, or a different word meaning the same thing. And when a man has been regenerated, is renewed, made over, recreated, born anew, born from above, born again, what actually happens to him?

Radical Life Change

When religion ceases to be a game and becomes a serious reality, when instead of playing a game he is fighting a war, then the Word of God has come in power and a number of things happen.

New Priorities

He is immediately changed *from the external to the internal*. Our trouble is externality. Automobile manufacturers keep poor automobile owners on their toes by just changing one little button inside the car so that the fellow has an old button. "This is just a year old, but I've got to trade it in." It is external. If your house has one level and you have a friend who has a split-level, you are worried until you get a split-level.

The Word that comes to us in power changes us from the external to the internal. Our hopes, our interests, everything that we are absorbed with and involved in are internal instead of external. And we see the emptiness of the appearance of things that are formed.

Scriptures tell us that "the LORD seeth not as man seeth; for man looketh on the outward appearance, but the LORD looketh on the heart" (1 Sam. 16:7). And the new man sees the transcendence of things eternal and the descent of things temporal, what belongs to the earth. He sees the inadequacies of everything intellectual while seeing the value of things that are above. He does not have to have an education. He does not have to be cultured; he just has to be born anew. And when the Holy Spirit regenerates him, he sees this. The Holy Spirit shifts his interest into a new sphere—the kingdom of God. The love life shifts from self to God; he is dedicated now to the honor of another. He was once dedicated bitterly to his own honor, but now he is dedicated to the honor of God. And he is changed in this too. He used to desire social approval. He wanted to be approved by the people, and now that has all changed. He desires to be approved by God Almighty.

As long as a man is a natural man, he wants to be popular with the crowd; but when he is born new, he says, "I don't care so much now about the crowd, but I want to stand approved of God. I want God to say in that day 'this is my beloved child in whom I am well pleased'; and I can well afford to stand the angry attacks of the people if I can only keep right with God."

From Ownership to Stewardship

Another change is that his *attitude toward earthly goods* completely changes. He no longer feels that he is a proprietor, owning anything. He feels that he is a steward who just has something for the time being.

There is a big difference in your life when this change happens. It will not mean that you have any less, but it will mean that you will have a different attitude toward earthly goods. Some Christians have a God-complex, they are proprietors, they own the place, give God part of it and feel they have done God service. I suppose they have, but there are other people who are blessed and see it differently. They say, "O God, I am not a proprietor, I am a steward. This is all Thine, and I am serving Thee. And I don't give Thee an amount that's mine, I simply give you back what's Thine, and You let me keep enough to run my family and my business."

That is a not only a different attitude, but it is also the only right attitude. As long as we imagine that we own anything, that thing will curse us. As soon as we know that we own nothing, it is God's. That is what happens to a man when he becomes a Christian.

A New Moral Code

Another significant change is that a man receives and lives by a new moral code. I grieve over the situation that is loose in the earth these days. Missionaries going out, God bless them, are having to fight not the devil so much as changing standards. In the early days, a man used to go out and when a chief had nine wives, the missionary said, "Get rid of every one but the first."

Now they talk about culture. "Well, but it is contrary to their culture. We're trying to impose our culture on them." A case of downright adultery becomes excused now. The psychologists, psychiatrists, sociologists and professors have made sin cute and unreal, saying, "It is a different culture, that's all."

Sodom had a different culture, too. When a stranger came at night, they said, "Where are the men which came in to thee this night? Bring them out unto us, that we may know them" (Gen. 19:5). The angels of God smote the place and pulled Lot in and said, "We'll handle these." Later, fire came down from heaven and burned the whole thing to ashes.

If the gospel does not change a man, transform him and take the evil out of him, then he does not have the gospel in power. The gospel is a transforming power; otherwise you have a name to live and you are dead.

A certain gangster out in California heard about the Billy Graham campaign and decided to go and hear him. He showed an interest in the gospel and even talked to the evangelist. Finally, Mr. Graham said to him, "If you give your heart to Jesus Christ you're going to have to do some changing."

He said, "Am I going to have to give up my Jewish religion?"

Billy Graham said, "You are going to have to become a Christian."

Well, the man pounced out angry and never went back. He was not willing to give up his religion for Christ.

Some may say, "Well, tell him no, he doesn't have to change anything, just believe on Christ." Thank God, Billy did not do that. He lost a friend and made an enemy, but he kept his own garment clean on the thing.

A man who has really been born anew lives by a new moral code. He does not go to the psychiatrists, the psychologists, the sociologists or the anthropologists and say, "What do you think of the Sermon on the Mount?"

A Greek philosopher gathered around him a group of young men who believed in that philosopher completely. If he said something, it was so. No further discussion was needed. I never knew the philosopher I trusted that much, but I know a man I trust that much. "The angel . . . said unto her, The Holy Ghost shall come upon thee, and the power of the Highest shall overshadow thee: therefore also that holy thing which shall be born of thee shall be called the Son of God" (Luke 1:35).

I can trust Him. My moral code is Christ. Jesus said, "You've heard it said so and so, but I say unto you . . ." He said it, and that is our moral code. You do not go to the philosopher to find out what Schopenhauer thought about it. I do not care what that old scoundrel thought about it. I do not even care what Plato thought about it. Jesus Christ is the one who saves me. He is the one who transforms me. He the one who stands with bleeding hands, pleading for me. He is the one who shall raise me from the dead. He is the one who shall stand as my advocate above, as my Savior by the throne of love.

The man who is a Christian does not ask someone else, "Did Jesus Christ say that? Well, then, I'm going to obey it." In all things, he acts upon and lives it not in his public life only, but in his total life, in private as well as public. At any cost to himself he will follow Jesus Christ and carry his cross if he is truly born anew, regardless of the cost of property or cost in pain or even the cost of his life itself.

There is a danger of our falling short here. There are millions who have a name to live, but they are dead. You say they are the liberals. No, liberals do not have any name to live. They do not pretend to live. They say, "I do not believe in that stuff. I believe that you only must be good and fan the fires within you and love your brother; be nice and you will be all right."

I am not talking about liberals, I am talking about people who are supposed to be Christians and who have received the gospel but received it in word only. It has never come in power because it has none of the fruits of power about it.

Nobody thinks this could be true of himself. It will pay us to do some heart searching in this terrible hour. The only safe thing to do is to surrender to the power of the gospel. Surrender to the words of Jesus Christ for your life—at home, in your business life, your property life, your private life, your personal life, your secret life. Surrender all and do not let any area of your life, even if it's only as big as a postage stamp, belong to the devil. Give everything to Jesus Christ . . . *everything*.

You say, "It'll cost me my job." All right, God will find another job for you. "I have been young, and now I am old; yet I have not seen the righteous forsaken, nor his seed begging bread" (Ps. 37:25). Someone will also say, "But I'll get stuck in jail if I follow the Lord." All right, go to jail and sing as Paul and Silas did. "I'll lose property." All right, lose your property. It is better to live in a rented house and a poor one at that, than have a mansion on the avenue with questions and uncertainties and moral spots all over it. Far better to come clean and get right, pay up, confess up, than go along and cover up, having a name to live while being dead.

Remember, the Word can come without power and leave us with a name to live while being dead. But the Word can come with power to transform, change and regenerate, making the old things new and making us examples to the world. Which do you want?

And Can It Be That I Should Gain
By Charles Wesley (1707-1788)

And can it be that I should gain
an interest in the Savior's blood!
Died He for me? who caused His pain?
For me? who Him to death pursued?
Amazing love! How can it be
that thou, my God, shouldst die for me?

'Tis mystery all: The Immortal dies!
Who can explore His strange design?
In vain the first born seraph tries
to sound the depths of love divine!
'Tis mercy all! Let earth adore;
Let angel minds inquire no more.

He left His Father's throne above
(so free, so infinite His grace!),
emptied Himself of all but love,
and bled for Adam's helpless race.
'Tis mercy all, immense and free,
for, O my God, it found out me!

Long my imprisoned spirit lay,
fast bound in sin and nature's night;
thine eye diffused a quickening ray;
I woke, the dungeon flamed with light;
my chains fell off, my heart was free,
I rose, went forth, and followed Thee.

No condemnation now I dread;
Jesus, and all in Him, is mine;
alive in Him, my living Head,
and clothed in righteousness divine,
bold I approach th' eternal throne,
and claim the crown, through Christ my own.

Chorus
Amazing love! How can it be
that Thou, my God, shouldst die for me?

7

The Nature of God's Kingdom: Not in Words Only

For the kingdom of God is not in word, but in power.
1 Corinthians 4:1-21

Paul embraced his authority as the chief apostle from the Lord for several reasons, the main one being to receive and shape church truth. Paul had received the revelation directly from God in the way that Jesus told his disciples. Jesus said, "I have yet many things to say unto you, but ye cannot bear them now. Howbeit when he, the Spirit of truth, is come, he will guide you into all truth: for he shall not speak of himself; but whatsoever he shall hear, that shall he speak: and he will show you things to come" (John 16:12-13).

When Ananias prayed for Paul, he was filled with that same Holy Spirit (see Acts 9:17). Then he was appointed by the Lord to set up a system and quality of standards for the church. Perhaps most important of all, Paul was to show, by example, the Christian way. Paul said, "I sent unto you Timotheus, who is my beloved son, and faithful in the Lord, who shall bring you into remembrance of my ways which be in Christ" (1 Cor. 4:17).

Now the apostle Paul was having his authority challenged by schismatic men who came in teaching that Paul was not a real apostle, alleging that he never saw the Lord. Their argument was that the other apostles walked with Jesus, but this man Paul had never walked with Him; he came after Jesus had died and risen. They overlooked the vision Paul had of Jesus as "of one born out of due time" (1 Cor. 15:8). These schismatic men who were dividers of the church had to repudiate Paul's authority in order to establish their own. As far as Paul was personally concerned, it did not matter. He said, "But with me it is a very small thing that I should be judged of you, or of man's judgment: yea, I judge not mine own self" (1 Cor. 4:3).

Paul went on to say, "I do not even judge my own self. I'm in the hands of God" (see vv. 3-4). But he knew that if he was going to have any influence, he had to establish his authority. So he sent Timothy to straighten them out, and finally warned them, "I told you before, and foretell you, as if I were present, the second time; and being absent now I write to them which heretofore have sinned, and to all other, that, if I come again, I will not spare" (2 Cor. 13:2). Paul refused to listen to these schismatics, these puffed-up fellows. Isn't it strange that there is nothing new under the sun?

So many of us imagine that we are originals, but there is nobody original except Adam. And if you find "puffers uppers" and men who are puffed up now, Paul wrote, "Now some are puffed up, as though I would not come to you. But I will come to you shortly, if the Lord will, and will know, not

the speech of them which are puffed up, but the power"
(1 Cor. 4:18-19).

The Form Is Not the Essence

Here is what I particularly want to emphasize: The kingdom of
God does not lie in words. I am among the few who are trying
to tell the Church that today. There are a few that see it, but not
very many. We see the word by the form of truth. Words are
only the outward image of truth and can never be the inward
essence. Words are incidental.

If I were to say, "Everybody who can speak Swedish, bring
your New Testament next Sunday to church; and everybody
who speaks German, bring yours. Any Norwegian, bring yours."
And so we would have half a dozen different languages. I would
say, "Now read the fourth chapter of 1 Corinthians." It would
be quite a revelation to hear that the words were only incidental, that it was the meaning that mattered. Somewhere in the
middle of this difference in words there is a spiritual meaning.
Six different people would embody that meaning in six different sets of words, and those were not alike or only occasionally
alike. We ought to remember that.

The kingdom of God is not in words. Words are only incidental and can never be fundamental. When evangelicalism
ceased to emphasize fundamental meanings and began empha-
sizing fundamental words, and shifted from meanings to
words and from power to words, they began to go down hill.

There is an essence of truth, and it may follow the form of
words as the kernel in an English walnut follows the conforma-
tion and configuration of the shell. But the shell is not the

kernel and the kernel is not the shell; and so while the truth follows the form of words, it sometimes deserts it. There is great heresy in holding the form to be essence and putting the kingdom of God in words so that if you have the words right you have the whole thing, and if you can get a better set of words, you have more truth. This is not necessarily true.

Words deceive even good honest Christian people. We feel that there is certain safety in mumbling words. Some believe there is power to frighten off Satan by mumbling certain words. Would you tell me, please, why the devil should be afraid of words? The devil, who is the very essence of ancient, created wisdom and had the perfection of beauty and the fullness of wisdom, and whose power lay in his shrewdness and intellectual prowess—can you tell me how that devil should suddenly become so foolish as to be afraid of a word or a motion or a symbol?

To keep the devil away, I put a chain around my neck or make a motion with my fingers in front of my face. I wonder what a man without any arms would do—what would an amputee do if the devil came after him and he could not make a sign of the cross? But the devil is not afraid of words or symbols. You can surround yourself with symbols, religious symbols, Protestant or Catholic or Jewish, but you have not helped yourself in the slightest, because the devil is not afraid of a symbol. He knows better.

Did you ever see a little child that is afraid of a false face? Put a mask on and the child runs and yells. If the child did that at 16, you would be ashamed of him. As soon as we grow up, we know that false faces do not mean anything and words do not mean anything as words. We imagine that if we say certain words, we will have power to bring good. If we say certain other words, they have power to fend off the devil, and there is safety in mumbling those words. If we fail to mumble the words, we are in for it, and if we remember to mumble the words, we are all right. That is just paganism under another form. It's just a religious veneer at best.

The Greeks loved oratory; they loved fine language and produced a lot of fine literature. Paul said, "You Greeks love fine words," but he said, "For I determined not to know any thing among you, save Jesus Christ, and him crucified. And I was with you in weakness, and in fear, and in much trembling. And my speech and my preaching was not with enticing words of man's wisdom, but in demonstration of the Spirit and of power: that your faith should not stand in the wisdom of men, but in the power of God" (1 Cor. 2:2-5).

We ought to throw this off as being superstitious and not Christian at all. A person may feel a little bit mentally naked when he throws all this off. When you strip superstition away from a man, he feels terribly naked for a moment; but until we strip off our superstition, the Lord cannot put on us a cloak of truth.

The Power Behind the Words

The kingdom of God lies in power; its essence is in power. The gospel is not the statement that "Christ died for our sins according to the scriptures." The gospel is the statement that Christ died for our sins according to the Scriptures *PLUS* the Holy Ghost in that statement giving it meaning and power. Just the statement itself never will do it.

Some churches drill their young people from childhood in the catechism and teach them doctrine so that they are positively instructed in the words of the truth. Somehow, they strangely fail to get them through to the new birth. A whole generation of so-called Christians drilled in the catechism, and who know doctrine and can recite the gospels as well as the law, still never manage to break through to the new birth. They never come through that shining wonder of inward renewal. The reason is, they are taught that the power lies in the words and if you get the words, you are all right.

Paul alleged, "The kingdom of God does not lie in words at all. The kingdom of God lies in the power that indwells those words, and you cannot have the power without the words; but you can have words without the power." And many people do have words without power.

It is the power of the Spirit operating through the Word that is the gospel. It is the statement that Christ died for our sins according to the scriptures, that He rose again, that He was seen of many, and that He is at the right hand of God and will forgive those that believe on Him. That is the gospel in its shell; but the power must lie in there or there will be no life in it.

Paul appealed away from man-given authority. He appealed away from talk, however eloquent, and even from his own position. He appealed directly to the power of the risen Lord manifested through the Spirit. And he said, "I want you to know and I sent Timothy to try to straighten you out and to remind you that it's the power of God that talks, not a man's mouth."

Paul's appeal was to the power of the risen Christ. If the evangelical church and the people who compose it are not living in a constant miracle, they are not Christians at all, because the Christian life is a miracle. It is what the Ark of Noah was in the day of the Flood. It was completely separated from the flood and yet floating upon it. It was what Jesus was when He walked among men, right in the middle of them yet separate from sinners. There operates within the true Body of Christ a continual energizing of the Spirit that makes a continual miracle. The Christian is not somebody who believes only; a Christian is somebody who has believed in power.

Power to Expose Sin

The working of this power is a moral power. It has power to expose sin to the sinner's heart. Nobody will ever be truly saved until he knows he is a sinner; and nobody will ever know he is a sinner by simply threatening, warning or telling him. You can go to a man and say, "You are a sinner, you swear and lie and you are wrong, you are evil." He will grin, shake his head and say, "I know, I shouldn't do those things, but I guess we're all human." You have not convinced him. You can read Plato, Aristotle, Herbert Spencer and all the rest of the books of ethics and show him he is dead wrong, and he still will never know what it is to be a lost sinner. You can threaten him that if he does not look out and does not straighten out his ways, an atom bomb will get him, and you still have not convinced him. You have not told him anything he did not know.

However, "when the Holy Ghost is come," said Jesus, "he will convict the world of sin and of righteousness and of judgment" (see John 16:8). When Peter preached at Pentecost, the Scripture said, "They were pricked in their heart, and said unto

Peter and to the rest of the apostles, Men and brethren, what shall we do?" (Acts 2:37). That word "pricked" is a word stronger and deeper than the word "pierced," where they pierced the heart of Jesus with a spear. The words of Peter, in the Holy Spirit, penetrated like a spear, deeper than the spear penetrated the heart of Jesus on the cross and forthwith came water and blood.

The Holy Spirit is not something we can argue about or somebody about whom we can say, "Well, you believe your way and I'll believe mine." The Holy Spirit is an absolute necessity in the Church. There is a power in the Spirit, which can expose sin and revolutionize and convert and create holy men and women, and nothing else can do it. Words will not do it. Instructions will not do it. Line upon line and precept upon precept will not do it; it takes power to do it. This power is a persuasive power to convince, persuade and break down resistance. It is also a worship power creating reverence and ecstasy.

If we were to put statues all around and have candles burning and have beautiful Italian-made, glass-colored windows, and pictures of shepherds and altars and all of that, and I were to come in wearing a long black robe, you would have a sense of reverence. But true reverence is not created by beautiful windows (although I like to see them) or by symbols. Reverence is astonished awe that comes to the human heart when God is seen. I can imitate holy tones and try to be just as religious and ecclesiastical as I can be and, still, when it is all over, the feeling I get is psychological or ecstatic at best. But when the Holy Spirit came upon the Early Church, they durst not join themselves to them. The sinners fell on their faces and said, "God is in this place of truth." So there is a power to bring reverence, to excite ecstasy, to bring worship; and it lies in the Word when it is given in power.

Power to Exalt Christ

Then the power of the Holy Spirit brings the magnetic power to draw us to Christ, exalting Him above all else and above all others. We must demand more than correct doctrine, though we dare not have less than correct doctrine. More than right living, though we dare not have less than right living; more than a friendly atmosphere, though we dare not have less than a friendly atmosphere. We must demand that the Word of God be preached in power, and that we hear it in power.

In 1 Thessalonians, Paul said to them, "For our gospel came not unto you in word only, but also in power, and in the Holy Ghost, and in much assurance; as ye know what manner of men we were among you for your sake" (v. 5). When the Spirit of God through the Word is preached in power and is heard in power, then the objectives of God are wrought. Holy men are made holy, and sins forgiven, and the work of redemption is done.

The way to obtain this is through prayer, faith and surrender, the old-fashioned way; and I know none other. As God's people, you have every scriptural right to demand that you hear the Word in power, and if you do not hear the Word in power, you have a right to rise up and ask why. If you are hearing nothing but teaching, nothing but instruction, with no evidence of God in it, and the preacher cannot say, "I appeal to God" to say whether this is true or not; if this cannot be, then you have a right to demand that somebody preach that can.

On the other hand, every man who stands in a pulpit to preach has a right to expect that the congregation believe in power and are so close to God, so surrendered, so full of faith and so prayerful that the Word of God can work in power.

Fellowship in the Holy Spirit

It is amazing how religious social atmospheres can permeate a church so that it is hard to tell which is of the Holy Spirit and which is simply nice social contact. I believe both ought to be in the church, and I believe they both can. When the Early Church met and broke bread, they fulfilled both their spiritual communion and their social fellowship. Therefore, there is no reason why they cannot be fused. There is not any reason why the warm cordiality of social fellowship cannot be made incandescent with the indwelling Holy Spirit so that when we meet and shake hands and sing and pray and talk together, we are doing both. We are having social fellowship, thus the mighty union and communion of the Holy Spirit.

Let us be very careful that it is both. To try to destroy or prevent social contact and social fellowship is to grieve the Spirit, because the Spirit made us for each other and He meant that there should be social fellowship and friendliness together. He meant that we should break bread formally not only in a church but when we meet. He meant that we should know each other by our first names and have our social fellowships. He meant it, and the churches that have tried to destroy that succeed only in getting a lopsided and fanatical type of church.

But be very careful lest we mistake the one for the other. So let us have a friendly church, and let us have a morally right church, and let us have a church where correct doctrine is taught. But let us also have a church that any man can come here and say when he goes away, "I know the entrance I had unto you that I could preach unto you not in word only but also in power and in the Holy Ghost and in much assurance because you are of a kind of people that could take it." This is most important, for the kingdom of God lies not in words but in power.

Love Divine, All Loves Excelling
By Charles Wesley (1707-1788)

Love divine, all loves excelling,
Joy of heaven, to earth come down;
Fix in us Thy humble dwelling;
All Thy faithful mercies crown.
Jesus, Thou art all compassion,
Pure, unbounded love Thou art;
Visit us with Thy salvation;
Enter every trembling heart.

Breathe, O breathe Thy loving Spirit
Into every troubled breast!
Let us all in Thee inherit,
Let us find that second rest.
Take away our bent to sinning;
Alpha and Omega be;
End of faith, as its beginning,
Set our hearts at liberty.

Come, Almighty to deliver,
Let us all Thy life receive;
Suddenly return, and never,
Nevermore Thy temples leave.
Thee we would be always blessing,
Serve Thee as Thy hosts above;
Pray, and praise Thee without ceasing,
Glory in Thy perfect love.

Finish then Thy new creation,
Pure and spotless let us be;
Let us see Thy great salvation
Perfectly restored in Thee;
Changed from glory into glory,
Till in heaven we take our place,
Till we cast our crowns before Thee,
Lost in wonder, love, and praise.

8

THE CHARACTERISTICS
OF A CARNAL
CHRISTIAN

And I, brethren, could not speak unto you as unto spiritual,
but as unto carnal, even as unto babes in Christ.

1 CORINTHIANS 3:1

Some people think of a spiritual Christian as being a rather tragic, anemic, mousey, soft-spoken, gentle and harmless person who walks about with a permanent smile and cannot be roused to any kind of spiritual indignation. I do not find this to be the scriptural definition of spirituality. If so, then Jesus Christ, John the Baptist and John and Peter could not be said to be spiritual men.

The carnal Christian is regenerated but is carnal and spiritually imperfect, retarded in his development. It is possible to be spiritually retarded just as it is possible to be retarded in our physical, spiritual and mental development, having the characteristics of a baby. Paul uses the word "babe" in 1 Corinthians 3:1, which is an anonymous description, such as the phrase "babes in Christ."

The church of Christ includes at least four classes. There is the average church person who comes all the time but never is converted. They come and seem to enjoy it and have friends among the Christian people, but they themselves have never passed from death unto life. That is one class.

There is another class, those who are trained to be Christians but are not. They appear as Christians because they have learned the language and are able to perform certain things, giving everybody the impression that they are in fact Christians. Usually, you find them in charge of all of the activities of the local church.

Then there are true Christians, but they are carnal. They have never developed into a mature, functioning Christian. They are where they were when they were saved.

Thankfully, there are also those who are true Christians and are spiritual. Unfortunately, this seems to be the minority in most churches.

What Typifies a Carnal Christian

I want to zero in on the carnal Christian. This seems to be the largest group in the contemporary church. They drain the church of power and influence while contradicting clear Bible teaching. Paul said those characteristics were unspiritual, they were carnal; and when those characteristics are in Christians, we find an unspiritual Christian. The best way to understand this is to compare the carnal Christian by noticing the characteristics of a baby.

Self-centered

Allow me to compare these carnal Christians with babies. Everyone is familiar with the delightful antics of babies. Personally, I love babies. In our home, we have had our share and then some of these delightful creatures. But the first thing I notice about a baby is its self-centeredness.

The baby has a little world all its own and has no idea there is any other world but its world. It is a self-centered little thing, and everything else—mother, father, brothers and sisters—revolve around that little central sun. All others are but bodies and are insignificant to the baby. He defines his world by "me," "mine" and other such phases.

This is Paul's concept of a carnal Christian, somebody that is self-centered, living a self-centered Christian life. He is born again, certainly, but living so that everything revolves around him. The only meanings others have are in relation to the baby's needs.

Feelings Oriented

Another characteristic of a baby is it is affected unduly by its feelings. A baby's quality of life revolves around its feelings. The slightest change in its feelings will have great repercussions on life in general. Every baby demands a perfect environment, which simply means one that complements his or her feelings. One moment he is a happy little fellow and the next moment is crying as though his world had ended. Evidence always gives way to feelings and emotions.

Normally, we draw a conclusion based on evidence rather than go along with feelings. Carnal Christians tend to live by their feelings. First, they must have what they call a good atmosphere in the church and then they have had a good time. If there is not a good atmosphere, they do not have a good time.

If this continues, they will look for a place more conducive to having a good time. They are more or less victims and fools of their environment.

A baby is a victim of its environment, a willing victim, because it hollers like a banshee when anything goes wrong. Although a baby's finger may stop hurting, he cries long after it is forgotten or no longer hurts, because it is unduly affected by its fears; or it is too hilarious and too humorous, for no reason in the world.

I discovered with our little granddaughter Judith that if I put my nose down on her nose and mumbled, she mumbled and would go into hilarious laughter, and we had a good time together. I wonder what is so funny about that? I do not know what is so funny about it, but she thinks it one of richest pieces of humor that had ever come to her little year-old circle of interest or attention. She and I do that now, that is our fun together. I do not think it is funny, but it is humorous to see her go wild about it.

Babies are either cast down for no reason or hilarious for no reason. They are victims of their feelings and senses, because they are carnal in faith. This also is the characteristic of a carnal Christian. He is too easily lifted up and too easily cast down. He cries when there is nothing to cry about and laughs when nothing is funny. After a while, a Christian should learn better.

Dependent on the External

A third characteristic about a baby is its propensity to rest in everything external. A baby has no inward life at all. Psychologists say that a baby is born without a mind; and as he grows, his mind develops. I do not know about that, but I do know that they are born with a capacity but without anything in their little minds. Give a baby a brightly colored rattle and it will entertain itself for hours. As they get older, the capacity develops, but they have no inward life. They rest completely in the external.

This also is characteristic of a carnal Christian. He lives too much in visible religion and goes by things on the outside. Colored lights, and strange or pretty sounds, and garments or certain uniforms or decorations; anything that feeds their childish mind by calling it out from the outside, from the internal to the external.

We may be as sure of this as we live that in proportion to the way we are affected by external circumstances, we are carnal. For Jesus said, "But the hour cometh, and now is, when the true worshippers shall worship the Father in spirit and in truth: for the Father seeketh such to worship him" (John 4:23). There is no other way the external can worship the Father perfectly. The carnal Christian cannot worship without religious rattles and toys; otherwise, he gets bored and loses interest.

For the mature Christian, any unlovely place is suitable for worship if the heart is right and the Spirit dwells within. Worship and communion with God can be real and can be unaffected, and the tranquility can remain the same, because the spiritual Christian does not rest in the external.

Without Purpose

Another characteristic of a baby is his complete absence of purpose. A baby sees a ball and wants it. He does not know what the ball is or what he will do with it once he gets it; but he wants that red ball that lies just beyond his reach. He has not yet learned to crawl and so he must howl for it, and when he gets it, he is let down. He did not want the ball for any purpose, and once he has it, no purpose would be fulfilled. That, of course, is characteristic of babies.

Sweet as they are, and I would not want them different—they are the loveliest things on earth—they lack purpose in life. But when a child gets a little older and starts crawling, he begins to say things, begins to put things away or starts to work toward something. By the time he reaches his teen years, he will have a life purpose worked out for himself.

Just as a baby has no purpose at all, I find that the carnal Christian has no purpose either. He lives for the next lesson. He wants to know where the good preacher is going to be and he goes to hear him. He wants to know where the fine choir is going to sing and he goes and sits down and tickles his carnality by listening to the finest choir he can find. Or he wants to know where the biggest crowd is assembled and he gets a charge out of the crowd. There is no purpose there; he never went aside and got on his knees and said, "God, why was I ever born, and why have I been redeemed, and what is this about?" His life is totally without purpose.

Unproductive

Then, a baby lives a life of playing with trifles. A baby is the most unproductive creature on the planet. We love them, but all they do is create work for their parents. They live a life of play and trifles altogether. Everything they do has to be turned into play. A baby will nurse on his bottle for a while, toss it out on the floor and then laugh hilariously when he sees the milk spill and the top come down on the rug. Everything has to be turned into play with the babies.

I am trying hard to be nice about this, but if you are realistic at all, you will have to say that the modern generation of Christians is living for play and trifles. I have a folder from a Bible conference advertising a trip out on top of the bounding billows on a luxury liner. They are going to have everything their hearts could wish. There are pictures of the beautiful palm trees and all the rest, like in Florida or California. It is going to be strictly a chaperoned luxury liner with a chaplain on board that will give talks on the Book of Romans just before the shuffleboard game every morning, to give it a religious flavor. According to the brochure, the purpose is to promote interest in missions. I did not get the connection. To me it would be more missions-wise to have everyone give that money to missions instead of spending it on the cruise.

Another group advertises, "Walk today where Jesus walked yesterday." I liked what a certain evangelist wrote: "Yes, but not with the same purpose."

We want to play and have no hesitation advertising our Bible conferences as religious playgrounds, which proves how carnal we are. We live a life of play and trifles. In order to get many Christians interested in Bible study or missions, it must be camouflaged as play to make it more palatable. A carnal Christian must be tricked into studying the Bible and it must be made out to be something that is fun.

Shifts Blame Away from Self

Another characteristic of a baby is that they are given to petulance, fretfulness and quarrelsomeness. A mother tells how her baby is a nice little angel. The mother means well, but that little girl is not a perfect little angel. She is a normal baby; she kicks and makes ugly sounds when she is only two months old. This petulance and fretfulness is strictly an immature reaction, because it is the temptation to blame secondary causes. All babies do it and eventually grow out of that stage.

I can always tell a carnal Christian because he blames secondary causes. When he loses his job, he blames his boss instead of blaming his sheer ineptitude and inability to come through. And some Christian women say that if only they had a good spiritual husband they would be better Christians. You know you would not be; you just think you would, because you would have fewer reasons.

As long as there is nothing there to think about, you think that you are better than you are. However, have a grouchy husband that will not shave on Sunday morning and sits around in a T-shirt and you say he is your trouble. No, he is not your trouble. He could be your sanctification if you knew how to use him. And if you knew how to use opposition, you could turn it into a help.

A carnal Christian always blames secondary causes. You never knew a baby that took the blame for anything; it is always somebody else that is at fault.

Eats a Limited Diet

A baby lives on a diet of milk and strained vegetables. Now, that is a picture of a baby. They are not yet able to digest solid food. Everything has to be processed to accommodate the delicate digestive system.

A carnal Christian marks his Bible from tender little passages and skips over those rough passages that tear you apart, bring you down, discipline you and chasten you. The carnal Christian is not able to handle the "meat of the Word." Everything must be predigested and given in measured doses so as not to offend their delicate digestive system. The apostle Paul addressed this in Hebrews 5:13-14, "For every one that useth milk is unskilful in the word of righteousness: for he is a babe. But strong meat belongeth to them that are of full age, even those who by reason of use have their senses exercised to discern both good and evil."

A carnal Christian and a baby share common characteristics: a self-centered little person affected by his senses; resting in the external; without any purpose; loving to play, and having no serious purpose in life; living on a simple diet. Well, there you have a baby. Nature takes care of a baby pretty soon. Nature begins to shift the baby out from the center, but not completely, of course; that is part of sin. The baby gets some interest away from itself and learns to stand up and defy the senses. It learns to reason instead of living by his senses; learns to live for the character within rather than for external things; learns to have a purpose in life even if it only is to be an actor or a ball player or something else. Having a purpose—nature takes care of that for most of us as we mature; but regarding spiritual things, that is another matter, dealing with fallen nature.

From Carnal to Spiritual

In spiritual things, what shall we do? How can a carnal Christian develop into a spiritual Christian? With the baby it is a natural development, but this is not so with the Christian. I know of no single experience that would instantly transform a carnal Christian into a spiritual one. I would like to be able to say that I do. I wish that I could say that I positively know how one can come to the Lord, meet certain conditions and cease to be carnal and become a spiritual Christian. It is simply not that way.

We must let the Spirit teach us, discipline us, mature us, grow big within us and walk within us; and we must learn by trial and error and prayer and repentance and fears and trials of hearts. Then we must believe in the power of God to fill us with His Spirit and begin to work with the soul, which leads us away from self-centeredness and leads us to love the whole world. The old saints used to sing, "I'll leave the world alone." They believed that the Christian ought to pray for the world but leave the world alone and follow Christ in surrender and self-denial.

Then, you have to tell God that you expect Him to teach you to live above your feelings and your senses. This is a difficult discipline in the Christian life.

Three young men from a religious institution in the Chicago area came to see me in my study. They were having a tough time of it. One was in trouble because when he got down on his knees, he didn't have any desire to pray. It troubled them, and they thought because I was an older Christian, I never had any difficulty like that.

In essence, I told them that there are times when I had to force myself to pray at all, and for a little while, there is not any peace in it. Their faces began to shine. One of them said, "Oh, what a relief! I thought I was backsliding because I had troubles like that."

There will be times when we will not feel spiritual, but we must pray through it. We have our fight down here, and we must learn not to trust in our feelings. When you get up in the morning feeling that you wish you had not, and in the evening you wish even more ardently that you had not, do not let that get you down. A baby will worry about that and holler for mother, but a grown-up Christian says, "Well, this was not my day."

No doubt, Paul had his days when things were not going right. So we keep our faith in God and Christ and know that no matter how we feel it is all right anyhow. A spiritual Christian stops resting in the external.

Mature Christians know why they are here. They know the purpose God put into their lives when He created them. I find myself sometimes so confused in my circumstance and so self-contradictory. If I did not know my Bible, if I did not know God and was not able to point back to certain markers where the stones were set up at the Jordan because it was God's blessing, I could easily blow my blessed ministerial top. But I do not do it, because I know that there are certain purposes I am fulfilling. So I have a purpose.

Carnal Christians have to have their religion turned into play. They drink a while, throw the bottle on the floor, laugh about nothing and get blue about nothing, which is carnality. Spiritual Christians have a life of labor; they look upon the world not as a playground but as a battleground.

And what about diet? A real Christian uses his whole Bible. This will make some of you mad, but if you are living on your morning daily devotions taken out of a book somebody compiled, I warn you that is pabulum. Read the entire Bible. Read it all. I do not say these other things are harmful, I just say that if you have that and nothing else, then you are not matured in your Christian life. Read all the Bible, read the "begats" and "begottens"; read it all.

A real Christian ought to be able to take a rounded diet. A spiritual Christian is a person who has grown up in God and is mature and growing in the Spirit. So let us ask God to make us mature Christians and grow in grace and in the knowledge of our Lord Jesus Christ.

Himself
By A. B. Simpson (1843-1919)

Once it was the blessing, Now it is the Lord;
Once it was the feeling, Now it is His Word.
Once His gifts I wanted, Now the Giver own;
Once I sought for healing, Now Himself alone.

Once 'twas painful trying, Now 'tis perfect trust;
Once a half salvation, Now the uttermost.
Once 'twas ceaseless holding, Now He holds me fast;
Once 'twas constant drifting, Now my anchor's cast.

Once 'twas busy planning, Now 'tis trustful prayer;
Once 'twas anxious caring, Now He has the care.
Once 'twas what I wanted, Now what Jesus says;
Once 'twas constant asking, Now 'tis ceaseless praise.

Once it was my working, His it hence shall be;
Once I tried to use Him, Now He uses me.
Once the power I wanted, Now the Mighty One;
Once for self I labored, Now for Him alone.

Once I hoped in Jesus, Now I know He's mine;
Once my lamps were dying, Now they brightly shine.
Once for death I waited, Now His coming hail;
And my hopes are anchored, Safe within the vail.

9

THE REMNANT: AN ALARMING DOCTRINE

*Esaias also crieth concerning Israel, though the number
of the children of Israel be as the sand of the sea,
a remnant shall be saved.*

ROMANS 9:27

I want to articulate a doctrine in the Bible that is very troubling
and alarming. I am very much afraid that the Bible is a more
alarming book than we know. Before I explain what I mean, I
would like you to read the words to a hymn. I love this hymn
from Edwin Hodder (1837-1904) about the Word:

Thy Word is like a garden, Lord.
With flowers bright and fair;
And everyone who seeks may pluck
A lovely cluster there.
Thy Word is like a deep, deep mine;
And jewels rich and rare

Are hidden in its mighty depths
For every searcher there.

Thy Word is like a starry host:
A thousand rays of light
Are seen to guide the traveler,
And make his pathway bright.
Thy Word is like an armory,
Where soldiers may repair,
And find, for life's long battle day,
All needful weapons there.

All of that is true. I enjoy hearing this song, and I enjoy singing it. However, I am a little bit afraid that that is the attitude we take toward the Scriptures—that it is a beautiful jewel to wear on or around our neck or our finger, or a corsage to wear at some dress-up occasion where the star shines on it; that it is fragrant. It is all that. But it is something more than that, and in our simple elegance, I am afraid we are not letting the Word of God mean to us what it ought to mean.

Whatever the educators may be saying, whatever the current religious vogue may be, here is the doctrine clearly taught in the Scripture, which cultists have misread and have wrested to their own destruction. For every cultist says, "I'm the remnant," and every group that meets says, "We are the people." But I refuse to reject the doctrine because somebody else has wrested the doctrine to his or her own destruction. I have neither starry hopes for you to admire nor posies for you to smell; but what I do have is a terrible doctrine that hurts and bothers and makes me sorrow in spirit. It is the doctrine of the remnant.

Only a Fragment

What is the doctrine of the remnant? It is simply this: that in our blind, fallen, sinful world of mankind, at any given time, the vast overwhelming majority is lost. And by lost, I do not mean they have missed their way or come short of the mark or are less than they wanted to be or fail to fulfill their dreams. By lost, I mean, alienated from God and an enemy to Him, without pardon, without life and without hope.

What does this doctrine of the remnant mean? "Remnant" means a small fragment, a surviving trace. It means that something yet remains when the larger body is somewhere else. The Romans 9:27 text deals with Israel, but it sets forth clearly the doctrine as applying to the entire human race as well as the Church. This was true among the nations before Abraham; it was true of Israel after Abraham; and it is true of the Church since Pentecost. I am alarmed because it has been true since Pentecost that such a vast number of people who call themselves Christians—the overwhelming majority—are nominal, and only a remnant is saved.

Look at some examples in the Bible. Jesus said, "And as it was in the days of Noe, so shall it be also in the days of the Son of man" (Luke 17:26). According to the Scripture, Noah found grace in the eyes of the Lord, and there were seven other members of his family that were saved out of that whole population. I do not know what the population was, but I know at the time of the Flood that there were eight persons saved out of a whole population. And I know that it is written that as it was in the days of Noah so shall it be in the days of the coming of the Son of man.

Somebody says, "Mr. Tozer, you're taking it too seriously. Don't you remember when Elijah felt the way you feel and Elijah said, 'Oh, Lord, I alone am left,' and God said, 'Cheer up, Elijah; I have news for you. Seven thousand are in Israel that have not bowed their knees to Baal nor to his image.'" That sounds like a lot. Isn't that encouraging knowing that in Israel 7,000 true Jews did not bow their knees to Baal?

Allow me to indulge in a little speculation. Suppose the population of Israel at that time was 7 million. I think that is a very conservative count. That would mean one tenth of 1 percent had not bowed their knees to Baal, and all the rest had. It would mean 1 in 1,000. If you were to take at that time 1,000 Jews, 999 of them were secretly bowing the knee to Baal to keep out of trouble, and only one man stood boldly.

But suppose for the sake of absolute fairness we cut the population of Israel in half, and say there were only 3.5 million. Then the ratio is 1 in 500. Every time you saw a synagogue or a building with 500 Jews reading the Torah or listening to the chant of the priests, you had 499 secretly following Baal and 1 that was saved.

Remember, at Christ's first coming there were only a few that recognized Him. We take it for granted, just as Israel did, that when Messiah came they would know it.

They believed just what Samson believed when he went to sleep in the lap of Delilah. He believed that he was well set for life and that he had some experience in religion, and therefore there was nothing to worry about. But when he woke up, he found that he had been captured, and his eyes were soon put out, and he was grinding at the mill and they were making sport of him in the name of a false god. He took himself for granted, which always is a bad and dangerous thing to do.

Either we take ourselves for granted and have a sham peace or we get disturbed and then pray through and find true peace. Most believers today take themselves for granted and have a false peace. If they did what the Bible taught, they would be bothered and alarmed about themselves and would go to God with an open Bible and let the Bible cut them to pieces and put them together again, then give them peace. And the peace they had when they had been chopped to pieces by the Holy Spirit and by the Sword of the Spirit—that peace, then, is a legitimate peace.

There are two kinds of tranquility, and do not forget it. Well, maybe there are three kinds now. There's the kind that you buy in bottles, and then there's the kind that you get from taking yourself for granted and believing good things about yourself that are not true. That brings a certain tranquility to the mind.

Then there is the tranquility that comes following a disturbance of the soul that shakes it to its foundation and drives the man or woman to God with an open Bible to cry, "Search me, O God, and know my heart: try me, and know my thoughts" (Ps. 139:23). Then when God does that, we have an experience with God that gives us a tranquility grounded upon the Rock. But with most evangelical Christians today, their leaders go outside to bring them tranquility.

The Tranquilized Church

The first offer from the Lord is not tranquility at all. The Lord at first offers us deliverance, forgiveness, renewal and making things right; and following that comes tranquility. But we are marketing tranquility now, selling it like soap, and asking our people in the name of John 3:16 to come and get tranquilized. And so we have a tranquilized Church that is enjoying herself immensely at banquets and times of fun and coffee-klatches and fellowships. Then she is singing about the Lord, "Thy Word is like a garden, Lord."

I only call attention to it because there is danger that we make the Word of God to be something to give us tranquility. The wings of the churches, the ones that are left open all day in the busy sections, you will find people come in and sit down. They do it, as the poet said, "To invite their souls and call in their thoughts of home and abroad and get still."

Businessmen and advertising men do that, and mystics from India and from Burma do that. That is not necessarily a Christian thing. It is a good thing, but it is not enough. We gear our services to tranquilize people and paralyze them. We ought to be alarmed by this doctrine of the remnant. We ought not to allow ourselves to take ourselves for granted. We ought to be alarmed about it.

Paul was troubled about this and wrote, "But I keep under my body, and bring it into subjection: lest that by any means, when I have preached to others, I myself should be a castaway" (1 Cor. 9:27). I have known preachers that preached a lifetime and ended up telling dirty stories—ending up being dirty, filthy old men. It is entirely possible for us to teach Bible school and be board members and sing in choirs and take part in church services and then finally find out that we are castaways and have never been of the remnant at all. That is an alarming thing, but I do not apologize for alarming you. I am afraid that we are not alarmed enough. We ought to be disturbed about this, for it is summed up in the text, "Though the number of the children of Israel be as the sands of the sea, a remnant shall be saved" (Rom. 9:27).

There were a few old friends of God during Jesus' time, but when we think that the population of Jerusalem alone at the time of the Passover was a million, and that at Pentecost there were also a million people in that city but only 3,000 were converted, we say, "What a vast harvest that was." Well, 3,000 out of 1 million is not a vast harvest, in my opinion.

I wonder if there has ever been a time when there was a vast harvest. I know it was said of Scottish missionary John G. Paton (1824-1907) that he went to the New Hebrides and found not a Christian; and when he left, there was not a heathen. But I have always crossed my fingers when I read that statement because it is not according to the doctrine of the remnant. For the doctrine of the remnant is "though the number of the religious people should be as the sands of sea, only a remnant shall be saved." It is not that they could not be, it is not that God does not want them to be, it is just that they are not.

When Christ came, there were shepherds and wise men. And we hear about these friends of God, we are glad for them. But the point is, they were typically a small percentage of the whole.

Well then, at the second coming of Jesus, He says, "And because iniquity shall abound, the love of many shall wax cold"

(Matt. 24:12). It does not say the love of many only, but every student of the Greek will tell the same thing. There is an article, a positive definite article in there: "the." The specific ability to love shall wax cold.

And Jesus said, "Nevertheless, when the Son of man cometh, shall he find faith on the earth?" (Luke 18:8). He did not say that He will not find faith, but He said, "Shall he find faith on the earth?" So at the second coming of Christ, it will be as it was in the days of Noah; and in those days, Noah, the eighth person, was saved by water, by the ark. The rest of the population drowned.

If you still want more support for the doctrine, read Church history. A small fragment, a surviving trace, always kept the faith while the others took things for granted.

Known by Their Fruit

Do you know what is wrong with us as a church today? We are taking ourselves for granted. We are assuming that which may not be true at all; that which is founded upon wishful hoping and not upon sound biblical experience in many cases. We have not been disturbed enough. We have not allowed God to plow furrows on our backs. We have not dared go before God and have the examination made. We have been afraid of what God will find, and we would rather wait. Therefore, we have waited and settled down. There has always been a small remnant, and they have been in the midst of all the rest. A million might wish with their lips and worship with their lips, but only a small fragment truly worship in their hearts in a way that honors and pleases God.

We do not need to imagine it is an indication of vast spirituality or high degree of holiness when we see a church door open and multitudes spew out on the sidewalk. Follow them home. Follow them a half a block and see how they live. That is the way to tell. "Wherefore by their fruits ye shall know them" (Matt. 7:20).

Ask them to lead in prayer. Announce a prayer meeting and see how they will leave. Announce a banquet and see how they will come. In the church of God, the "stop and go" signs are these: When it says go, "banquet"; when it says stop, "prayer meeting." The church of God follows it, and we smile about it, but it is an alarming thing. I do not want to come before the Lord having soothed and petted people into some false sense of smug spiritual security.

Read Church history and see the fragments, or the remnant, that lived in the midst of it all. Read about the Waldensians and the Friends of God and the Brethren of the Common Life and how few there were but how many went to church. It is possible to worship God with our lips and not worship God with our lives. If your life does not worship God, your lips do not worship God either.

I am troubled about all the people I see singing Handel's *Messiah*, especially during Easter season, without having the remotest notion of what it is about. They will stand up and sing, "Come unto Him, come unto Him," and they will not have any idea of what it means. When Handel wrote it he said, "When I was through, me thought I saw heaven open and all the angels of God gathered." That is how he felt. But many of us sing it and only enjoy it as music. We can come, sing hymns in church and only enjoy the dignity of the music as a relief from rock 'n' roll.

Read about the remnant 600 years before Christ was born in Ezekiel 9:1-6. We say, "Begin in the Kremlin, O God; begin in the Kremlin and destroy those godless wretches." God says, "Begin at my sanctuary."

We say, "Go down to the corner where men in half-lighted rooms sit and slurp beer; go down there, oh ye with the destroying weapon in your hand." God says, "Begin at the steps of my church. Begin with my sanctuary."

We say, "Go to the church where the pastor denies the Bible and has nothing to preach but poetry." God says, "Begin at my sanctuary."

But He says, "Look out, watch for the mark on the forehead." That indelible mark. He sent the man with the linen with an inkhorn, indelible ink, and said, "Go mark them, mark them."

"Which ones will I mark? The ones that stand and pray the longest? The ones that give the most to missions?"

"No, no," He says, "that is not the test. Here is the test in a day of corruption: those who sigh and cry for all the abominations that are coming in the midst of Jerusalem."

That is all that they have to do. Some things are like a wave of the sea. You can stand, and Paul himself could not shout it back, for it would engulf him. But you do not have to get the mark of the remnant on your forehead, you do not have to succeed, and you do not have to be popular. You only have to sigh and cry for the abominations that are taking place in the earth today.

I cannot stop people from doing what they are doing, but at least I can grieve because they will not stop; and I am going to do that. I am going to let my tears water the footsteps of those who go astray. And when the churches will not come back to New Testament standards and worship the Lord our God in the beauty of holiness, if I cannot make them do it or persuade them to do it in this awful hour of crisis, at least I can weep because they will not come. And I can sigh if I cannot weep.

I do not know what the future holds. But I know one thing: Rather than betray the sheep of God, rather than lie to them and deceive them and keep them agitated and stirred up with all kinds of popular topics; rather than take my material from *Time* magazine, I'll preach the Word to empty seats and sigh and cry for the abomination that is in the earth.

So God says, "Begin at my sanctuary. Then they began at the ancient men which were before the house" (Ezek. 9:6). Sounds like these young people are the trouble. These young people are filled with lust and wild ideas; but the Scripture says, begin with the ancient men, which are before the house. "These old bearded pillars of the church," says the Holy Spirit, begin with them. "And it came to pass, while they were slaying them, and I was left, that I fell upon my face, and cried, and said, Ah Lord GOD! Wilt thou destroy all the residue of Israel in thy pouring out of thy fury upon Jerusalem?" (Ezek. 9:8).

If the evangelical Church, the fundamentalist believing Church, will not accept this, then I can at least sigh because they will not, and cry to God because they do not.

Fully Surrendered

By Alfred C. Snead (1884-1961)

Fully surrendered—Lord I am Thine;
Fully surrendered, Savior divine!
Live Thou Thy life in me;
All fullness dwells in Thee;
Not I, but Christ in me,
Christ all in all.

10

THE SACRED OBLIGATION OF JUDGING

For he will finish the work, and cut it short in righteousness:
because a short work will the Lord make upon the earth.

ROMANS 9:28

Where is the remnant? Where can we find them? As soon as we bring this subject up, immediately all of the half-saved and the one percent saved—the backsliders, the borderline, the church members, the professors and those who have no witness of the Spirit to their redemption—begin to squirm and quote Scripture. And one Scripture they quote is, "Judge not, that ye be not judged" (Matt. 7:1).

They say, "That man is an old bigot, and he judges other people's religion, and he judges me. What right has he to judge me? Does not the Bible say that love 'thinketh no evil' (1 Cor. 13:5)? And if that man had love, he would not think evil about anybody. He would accept everything done in the name of the Lord and would not say, 'Only a remnant shall be saved.' He would accept and believe in the good religious people that go and give of their pennies, and he would believe in them. But he's not a loving man; he's a severe, harsh man."

I wonder if when Jesus said, "Judge not," and when Paul said, "Love thinketh no evil," and when Christ said that we should love one another and lay down our lives for each other, if that was intended to end inquiry and silence rebuke? I wonder if Jesus meant, when He said, "Judge not that ye be not judged," that His prophets, His apostles and His preachers were not to go forth and speak truth to the church? I wonder if he meant that they were to go forth like the three monkeys on the whatnot shelf, "see no evil, think no evil, hear no evil," and get the permanent smile on their faces that never will rub off until they die? I wonder if He meant they were to go forth believing in everything and everyone who says, "Lord, Lord," and accept them into the kingdom of God? Did He mean forgetting that the same Holy Ghost who said, "Judge not," through the lips of the Savior said a "remnant shall be saved," a small fragment, a surviving trace?

Diagnostic Dilemma

Do you know what we need in the evangelical church now? We need diagnosis. Do you know what "diagnosis" is? It comes from two hard Greek words meaning to know all the way truth. That is what we need in the church of Jesus Christ.

Suppose somebody isn't feeling up to par and goes to see his doctor and says, "Doctor, I feel as if I have a mitten in my mouth when I get up in the morning, my head has bothered me and I don't have energy and I just don't feel good."

And the doctor says, "All right, stick out your tongue."

The patient looks at the doctor with a puzzled look and says, "What?"

"Put out your tongue."

"I can't understand why you should want me to put out my tongue."

"Well I've got to know you all the way through; I've got to diagnose you, get to know you."

And the patient says, "It's an improper thing to do, and I beg your pardon."

"Well," the doctor continues, "how's your appetite?"

"I don't see why that's any of your business."

"Well, how do you sleep?"

"What difference is it to you how I sleep? I came for help; don't you love me? I want you to help me, but don't you love me?"

"Yes, but I want to know, do you sleep well at night?"

"None of your business, doctor. You're a terrible man. Don't you know the Scriptures say, 'Love everybody, judge nobody, love thinketh no evil and love covers a multitude of faults'? And don't you read the New Testament? Asking me how I sleep . . . none of your business."

"Well, let me take a little bit of your blood."

"My blood?!"

"Yes."

"What do you want with my blood?"

"I want to know you through and through."

"I came for help. I want encouragement and inspiration. I don't want to give up my blood."

"I can't know you until I see your blood."

"Oh, you are terrible, and you're a radical bigot. Why should you want to know about my blood?"

"Well, let me at least take your blood pressure."

"What do you want to know about my blood pressure? It is none of your business. Do you not realize that the Bible says, 'Thou shalt not judge,' and if you take my blood pressure, you'll be judging me?"

A Lack of Diagnostic Preaching

What kind of a crazy business would that be between doctor and patient? Satan would hold his belly and laugh in hell. Yet we demand that is the way the preacher is to feed the congregation.

I want to tell you something: We are beating the drum for revival and we are getting thousands of people to pray into the night for revival. But we might as well jump up and down on the altar of Baal, cut ourselves and cry, "Baal hear us, Baal hear us." We will not submit to diagnosis. We will not let God find out what is wrong with us. We will not let God know us through and through, and we will not listen to the man who tries to find out and minister to our needs.

We go to the preacher for inspiration and encouragement and confirmation in our backslidden ways. As soon as he opens his mouth, even if he prays half the night for his congregation and would give his life for it, we shut him up by ramming this text into his mouth: "Don't you dare judge anybody."

The man says, "I'm a Christian, and you've got to accept it, otherwise you might be grieving the Holy Spirit." And we shut up the mouth of the man who is trying to find out what is wrong and how we can be cured.

If this is true, that I am only to preach love, that I am only to tell you from the Book of Ephesians how wonderful you are, if that is true, then all the prophets who spake since the world began are all wrong. Beginning with Enoch, who said, "Behold, the Lord cometh with ten thousands of his saints, to execute judgment upon all, and to convince all that are ungodly among them of all their ungodly deeds which they have ungodly committed, and of all their hard speeches which ungodly sinners have spoken against him" (Jude 1:14-15).

That does not sound much like inspiration and encouragement and moving on to better things. Sounds to me more like a little diagnosis. It sounds to me like somebody getting into it to find out what is wrong.

If I do not dare to diagnose, and you will not listen to it, then all the prophets were wrong. And Christ was the greatest transgressor of them all. For there was nobody that could look you through and through and make you feel like two cents devalued. Nobody could do it as well as our Lord Jesus Christ could.

And if that is the way it is and all inquiry must be ended and all rebuke silenced, then the apostles were also great sinners and great bigots and heretics. For if you do not believe it, read what Paul wrote to the Corinthians; read what he wrote to the Colossians; read what he wrote to the Galatians; read what Peter wrote to the general Christians scattered abroad; read what Jude wrote about the people that crept into the Church. Read what John wrote in his first epistle and all his epistles. Read what James said. Had not these men heard the text "judge not, that ye be not judged" (Matt. 7:1)?

Sure, they heard that text, but they knew what it meant.

Had Paul not heard the text "[love] thinketh no evil" (1 Cor. 13:5) when he said, "You lovers of Jewish circumcision are always trying to make Christians with a pair of scissors, I wish you'd get clear cut off he said, get rid of yourself, get out of the church"? He was the man who wrote this text that said "[love] thinketh no evil," and that love was the greatest thing in the world. And then he told the Galatians' false teachers, "Get out and cut yourself off."

It is time for diagnosis. It is time to inquire, to search, to get at the blood, to take blood pressure and find out what is wrong.

Should I tell you that the mystics were all wrong and the Reformers were all wrong, and Martin Luther should have been in jail, and Charles Finney should have spent a term or two in jail, and all of the men who have moved the world for God should all have been in jail?

If that is true, then it is also impossible to obey the Scriptures. Then I dare not exercise moral judgment; I dare not stand up and look at a thing and decide in the light of God's Word whether it is right and wrong. It means the Lord has given me a commandment that I cannot obey. "Beware of false prophets," He says, "which come to you in sheep's clothing, but inwardly they are ravening wolves" (Matt 7:15). And the modern theologians say, "Don't you judge anybody, but accept everybody at his own face value and be loving as the Savior was."

All right then, when the wolf comes along dressed in sheep's clothing, what do I do? Do I say, "Good morning sheepie"? Do I dare not allow myself to believe that he is a wolf, even though I see his slobbering fangs?

Nobody can get quite as effusively affable as these blind men who are afraid to preach the truth. "Be loving, dear brother," they say, and they paw you and call you "dear brother" with their soft white hands. If I am not to be able to identify a wolf when I see him, then how am I going to keep the wolf out of the fold like I am supposed to do? How can I beware of that which I do not dare identify, tell me?

Jesus said, "Wherefore by their fruits ye shall know them" (Matt. 7:20). Now, suppose I go out to an old rundown garden looking for a sheep-nosed apple, the kind we used to raise out in Pennsylvania, but all I can find is a crabapple and a thorn apple and a sour, dried-up, degenerative apple full of worms.

Somebody asks, "What are you doing, Reverend?"

"I'm out here judging fruit. I'm out here looking for fruit."

"Well, but you're not supposed to. Why, the Bible says, 'judge not' and you are not supposed to judge fruit, you are not supposed to do it. Doesn't Paul say, 'Love thinketh no evil,' and 'Judge not that ye should be judged,' and 'love everybody'? That poor crabapple is doing the best it can, and that thorn berry is trying to look like an apple—it's a sheep-nosed apple on the way up, if you would only believe it. Why, the Lord loves the dear thing, why should you be so hard on it?"

Therefore, I have to go sneaking away. I do not even dare know the difference between a great big gorgeous, juicy sheep-nosed apple and a crab apple. Because if I do, I am judging. You cannot obey the Scripture; you cannot obey the truth the Lord has given us. If you cannot exercise moral judgment, if you cannot criticize and discriminate, then you cannot obey what you have been told to do. The apostle John said, "Beloved, believe not every spirit, but try the spirits whether they are of God: because many false prophets are gone out into the world" (1 John 4:1). Why does he give us these words if we cannot and dare not try the spirits?

Should I be afraid to judge when God Almighty sent me to do it? Afraid to distinguish a crabapple from a sheep-nose apple when God sent me to do it? Afraid to look at a wolf and say, "You are a wolf," when God said, "Look out for wolves"? Afraid to try the spirits when God said, "Try the spirits whether they be of God"? God is not going to send me out to do something and then damn me for doing it. He is not going to send me out and say, "You go out and judge the fruit," and then damn me for judging fruit.

Scripture says, "Prove all things, hold fast that which is good" (1 Thess. 5:21), and if we cannot exercise moral judgment, then I want to know how we can know good from bad. The scriptural injunction is, if anyone that is called a brother commits fornication as well as any of these other things, idolatry and all the rest, do not eat bread with them. That is, do not have communion with him at the Lord's house. We are where we are because we have silenced the preachers who dared to find out what is wrong with us, who dared to inquire where the remnant is or even if there is a remnant.

Examine Yourself

What are we to do about it? First, let us be aware of something. Let us beware of presumption and self-righteousness. This is the snare of all cults and sectarians, and the Pharisees. Let us beware of the spirit that says, "I am right, judge yourself by me."

The wonderful thing about a right man is that he does not want to talk about it. The wonderful thing about a godly man is that he does not know he is godly. The beautiful thing about a holy man is that he is the only one who does not know it.

As soon as we begin to talk about how holy we are, we are not holy any more, if we ever were. If somebody else says a man is holy, I would listen; but if he gets up and says that he is, I close my ears right there, because I do not want the decibels to disturb the atoms inside my eardrum because I know he is not telling the truth. A good man does not know he is good, and a holy man is not aware that he is holy, and the righteous man thinks he is miserable. "Oh, I'm such a poor wretch. I love my Savior so, and I'm so happy in God, but when I think of myself it makes me sick."

What then is the right attitude? The right attitude is to refuse to compare yourself with anybody else. Compare yourself only with Jesus. The man who belongs to the remnant is not asking if he belongs to the remnant; he is hoping and believing and trusting and seeking and longing and comparing himself not with somebody else but with the Savior. Compare yourself with somebody else and you will be proud as Lucifer. Compare yourself with Jesus and you will be as humble and meek as Moses (see Num. 12:3).

So the thing to do is not look for the remnant; the thing to do is to beware of presumption and self-righteousness and to compare yourself only to Jesus. Then when you have done that say, "I am an unprofitable servant."

The point is, you are going to have to come to Him in meekness and humility and not say, "I am holy, stand thou aside," but say, "Lord God, I trust that by Thy grace and the power of the blood of the everlasting covenant, I may gain some little reward there; but I'm an unprofitable servant."

It is my opinion—I believe it is more than an opinion, it is insight—that evangelical Christianity as we know it is almost as far from God as liberalism. Its nominal creed is biblical, but its orientation is worldly. The modern evangelicals, the Holiness people, the Pentecostal people, the Bible loving people—we who claim to be evangelical and traditional in our Christian faith— have an orientation toward the big businessman. You know, Jesus never got along with any of the businessmen in His day. But we use them as our model.

Our orientation is around the banquet hall.

The evangelical church is oriented around showmanship. I can always tell who they are, and I smile to myself and pray that God would wake them up. When I hear a young man leap to the platform, I know where he has been; I know where he has been brought up. He leaps up almost vibrating, and he is an emcee. He learned that from TV. He knows how to smile that greasy smile he puts on with a paddle, and he drags that damnable thing into the church. He leaps up and announces the meeting: "And now Mabel Persnickety and Harry Jones will sing . . . all right, kids."

I know where he has been, and when I sniff, there is no aroma of myrrh, no aloes, no cassia, no fragrance of heaven. When I take a whiff, I know where he has been. His orientation is TV and movies. But he has a Bible as big as a cedar chest under his arm, and he carries it down the road and says, "I'm preaching a sermon five blocks long, carrying my Bible five blocks." Then he upsets the sermon by arriving at the church acting like a worldling.

We are oriented to play and toward being respecters of persons, of religious bigwigs. We are mousey and timid, and if one of these fellows swaggers down the aisle, the little preacher leaps to attention and salutes.

There is not a man in Chicago high enough in society or deep enough in debt or owning enough property or having enough bank accounts or able to write a big enough check to shut my little old mouth. Not one. He may be a priest of this or a cardinal of that or a bishop of the other. He may be the uncrowned potentate of fundamentalism or the self-appointed without portfolio ambassador of modern evangelicalism, but I will still preach what God wants me to preach.

Live Like the Early Church

So, what can we do? I think the first thing that we must do is return to New Testament living. We must get into the Scriptures and discover the level of morality and ethics that are the mark of true believers in Christ. We are to deny ourselves and forsake the world on every level possible and always keep in mind that Christianity and the world do not mix. You cannot have a Christian world, but unfortunately, you can have a worldly Christian.

Finally, we must resist the magnetism of the majority. We must never allow the majority to overrule the clear teaching of the Word of God. Then we can return to Jesus Christ as Lord and throw our loyalty and support to him and all those who follow Him.

I Would Be Like Jesus

By James Rowe (1865-1933)

Earthly pleasures vainly call me,
I would be like Jesus;
Nothing worldly shall enthrall me,
I would be like Jesus.

He has broken ev'ry fetter,
I would be like Jesus;
That my soul may serve Him better,
I would be like Jesus.

All the way from earth to glory,
I would be like Jesus;
Telling o'er and o'er the story,
I would be like Jesus.

That in heaven He may meet me,
I would be like Jesus;
That His words "Well done," may greet me,
I would be like Jesus.

Chorus
Be like Jesus, this my song,
In the home and in the throng;
Be like Jesus, all day long!
I would be like Jesus.

11

THE HAUNTING
MEMORY OF DEAD
WORDS

Thy word have I hid in mine heart, that I might not sin against thee.
PSALM 119:11

In every thought or endeavor at any given time in history certain words and phrases dominate. They govern the thinking and endeavors of that generation, within that field.

It is true in the field of philosophy, and it is true in the field of literature and politics and religion. In every generation, every age, every period in history, certain phrases, words and ideas become lords over the minds of men. They determine the direction of the endeavor of men in that generation. The power of these words lies in that they embody and express leading ideas.

Do not undervalue the power of an idea. John says, "In the beginning was the Word, and the Word was with God, and the Word was God. The same was in the beginning with God. All things were made by him; and without him was not any thing made that was made" (John 1:1-3). When John said, "In the beginning was the Word," he used the word *logos*. In the beginning was an active idea in expression. So in the beginning was an active idea, and everything was made out of that idea, born out of the heart of Jesus Christ the Son of God.

Everything that is round about us anywhere where men live grew out of an idea or ideas. Take civilization, for instance. It is so hard to understand that I do not know if I know what civilization is exactly, but it is certainly better than the jungle. It is better to live in the Jefferson Hotel than to live in a mud hut and sleep on the floor. Civilization has its points, and it began in the discontented mind of somebody way back yonder who determined he was going to fix things up a little bit and make things better. And so our civilization has come out of that idea.

Take the idea of *liberty*. There is still some left in this country, and all that we have that we see and have enjoyed over the generations came out of the idea of tortured minds of certain men, sometimes even in prison, who dreamed high dreams of liberty. Benjamin Franklin, Thomas Jefferson and the rest of the founding fathers embodied those ideas in the Constitution of the United States, the mightiest and noblest document, William Gladstone said, ever struck off by the mind of man. It all began with an idea.

So is the idea of *transportation*. Somebody, somewhere, wearing a leopard skin, discovered the wheel. He discovered that if you took a round thing and put a hole in the middle, you could easily roll it; and out of that was born the wheel. Out of the wheel came automobiles, airplanes, trains and everything else that takes us from one location to another.

Then *communications*. Guglielmo Marconi, an Italian inventor, was one of the first to develop a commercial, workable radio communication. It is supposed that he sent and received his first radio signal in Italy in 1895. Out of this idea came radio and television and what the English call wireless.

It is the same with *the Reformation*. A man named David, under inspiration of the Holy Spirit, said, "Blessed is the man unto whom the LORD imputeth not iniquity, and in whose spirit there is no guile" (Ps. 32:2). That idea went to sleep for a long time. It came to life again in the heart of the man Paul, and he gave us the Book of Romans and Galatians. The idea of justification by faith leaped into the thinking of the Early Church and then went to sleep again for a long time. It was brought to life again in the mind of the German man named Martin Luther, and some of his helpers, and we had the Reformation.

And it was out of the tortured heart of one man, Dr. A. B. Simpson, that the Christian and Missionary Alliance was born. It had to be an idea before it could be a society. So the whole Christian and Missionary Alliance, with its missionaries all over the world, once lay in the heart of a Canadian man named A. B. Simpson. It was an idea not as big as an acorn, scarcely so big that you could measure it, but it was there.

Ideas are mighty things. Never undervalue them. But there is a catch in this whole business; ideas, words and phrases have a way of living only one generation and then dying. After they die, however, they refuse to fade away; they still dominate after they are dead.

Dead Words in the Next Generation

In religion, we see this more clearly than in any other field of human endeavor or thinking. God will come along and give to a generation a living idea good for that hour, a living truth. This living truth will become clothed, incarnated, in a glimpse of a phrase or a word or half a dozen phrases. This phrase will get itself into a bibliography. It will have books written about it, magazines dedicated to it, preachers going up and down the country preaching it; and it will have schools gather around it and will become a school of thought in its generation. Because it is a living idea, and it came from the heart of God, it is alive, creative and powerful, and great things are born out of it. Then it will die. It will die in the heart of the people it helped to create, usually the next generation.

After that, it will continue to dominate. Those dead words and phrases that once described a living idea continue to determine our doctrine and how the preachers in that group will preach and what they will teach in the school and what they will get in the magazines and write in books and what they will sing. Nobody recognizes that the word died a generation ago. That word is bandied around by everybody, tossed around, and has become the catchword and center for great groups of people, denominations even. But that word died long ago and it had not any life left in it, and it does not do what it set out to do or did originally, It does not do what it did to the first or second generation that used it.

And so we continue for another generation or two to be dominated by the ghosts of theological words, those zombies of the tomb. We live with spectral voices that call out of the tombs of theology, out of the musty tombs where the dead lie. Nobody ever has the courage to challenge that and say, "This thing is dead," and look to God for a live idea. And so we have the great dead hands of theological phrases choking us. Our lifeblood is being choked out by the continual use of words that once meant something still to some people but do not mean anything to us.

Dead Words in Today's Church

I am going to name only two of these dead words. One of them is the word "accept." This word teaches *the doctrine of moral passivity.* The other word is "receive," which teaches *the doctrine of spiritual quiescence.*

"Accept" was a good word at one time. Incidentally, the word "accept," in the sense of "accept Jesus," does not occur in the Bible. But there was a time when it was a living idea. It described a set of circumstances with spiritual experiences and conditions being what they were in a given generation. Living voices rose and said, "You're not saved by works, you're saved by accepting Christ," and there was life to it. Men who had been trying to climb to heaven on Jacob's ladder of good works suddenly discovered that they could accept Him into their heart and be converted like that. It was a wonderful word in its day.

In the great campaigns of a former generation, it became the catchword for evangelicalism, fundamentalism, full gospelism and world missions. It contained a mighty truth that has long since died, but the word stays on. It stays on the theological spectrum and is producing a generation of Christians, or so-called Christians, that are impenitent in their hearts, frivolous in their spirits and worldly in their conduct. Telling people who come to us to be converted, "Accept Jesus," and so they say, "All right, I'll accept Jesus." So they accept Jesus and that is about all there is to it. There is no transformation and no impenitent root of their being that is ever cured. There is pride that has never been crucified, a worldliness they have never been able to deal with and a frivolity of spirit that is beyond description. There is a whole generation running around today that are the victims of this dead theological word "accept."

To give you an illustration of what I mean, there is one place that specializes in reaching out to young men in the service and talking to them about the Lord. They have a staff that is supposed to witness to them of the Lord Jesus before they go overseas.

One day, one of their workers, a Baptist preacher, came to me in my study. He threw himself down on a little old davenette and said, "Brother Tozer, I'm in agony. I'm working at such-and-such center. Do you know what the trouble is down there? They will not let me mention repentance. All I can dare tell the boys going out to die is that they accept Jesus. The result is that they bow their heads and say, 'Yes, I accept Him,' get up with a sort of smile in a pitiful way and shake my hand. Some of them are scared kids, on their way out. They may not come back, and I don't even dare talk to them about repentance of life or sin, or of sorrow for sin. I'm bound to say only to accept Jesus."

The damage of this will be seen in future generations when the Church will be anemic and worldly oriented in all aspects. To "accept" Jesus and not demand a transformed man or woman will result in actually rejecting the Christ of the New Testament. All over the country, evangelists are blazing abroad the message "accept Jesus," which has become in our day nothing more than a theological zombie, a voice out of the tomb that means nothing to this generation.

The second word is the word "receive." That word teaches *the doctrine of spiritual quiescence.* Both "accept" and "receive" are passive words, and the outworking of this receive doctrine is nothing short of a tragedy in our country.

When I was a young man, I happened to get into the company of an elderly woman, God bless her memory. She did not have too much theology. But she believed that the way to get filled with the Holy Spirit was to get down on your knees and die out and open your heart. Not having very much theology either, at the time, thank God, I obeyed. The result was an old-fashioned mighty invasion of my nature by the Holy Spirit. That is why I cannot preach any sermon without mentioning the Holy Spirit and the baptism of the Holy Spirit, because I received that baptism.

It was not long after that time that the church began to say, "Receive the Holy Spirit." Some hungry-hearted, pensive-looking young fellow would come and ask, "How do I receive the Holy Spirit?" and his teacher would say, "Why receive, just receive Him, young fellow. Do you receive Him?"

"Yes, I receive Him."

The tragedy is that that young fellow, and others like him, did not receive Him. And we have sent men out by the dozens, even to the mission fields, that have nothing any better than the doctrine of spiritual passivity.

These are dead words, though in another set of circumstances, at another moment, they may again leap to life and become the very words of God for a generation.

The Danger of Dead Words

Those words, "accept" and "receive," have been abused and allowed to die, and they have died in the house of their friends. The result is that we do not receive, and whatever kind of belief we have does not change our life.

I once received a long-distance call from a woman living in Boston. She said, "I just finished reading *Divine Conquest*, and my husband and I want to come to Chicago and be filled with the Holy Spirit."

"Well," I said to her, "you don't have to come here to be filled with the Holy Spirit."

She said, "Now, wait a minute, I don't know anybody in this city that will tell me how to be filled with the Holy Spirit."

I did not know where to tell her to go; I suppose there were people that could help, but you cannot talk for too long over a phone. I said, "Sister, I can't have you come here."

I said, "You go and read *Divine Conquest* on your knees, both of you, and keep on reading it until the fire falls."

She said, "Do you think that will work?"

I said, "That'll work all right."

I do not know what happened, but I trust that is what happened.

Many other words could be illustrated as being dead to this particular generation of Christians, but the words "accept" and "receive" are destroying the very nature of the Church. If something is not done to correct this, the next generation of Christians will suffer from deep spiritual maladies that will keep it from being the testimony to their generation that God fully intends them to be.

Wonderful Words of Life
By Philip P. Bliss (1838-1876)

Sing them over again to me,
Wonderful words of life;
Let me more of their beauty see,
Wonderful words of life;
Words of life and beauty,
Teach me faith and duty:

Christ, the blessed one,
Gives to all,
Wonderful words of life;
Sinner, list to the loving call,
Wonderful words of life;
All so freely given,
Wooing us to heaven:

Sweetly echo the gospel call,
Wonderful words of life;
Offer pardon and peace to all,
Wonderful words of life;
Jesus, only Savior,
Sanctify forever,

Our dear Savior will come some day,
Wonderful words of life;
Come to rapture His Bride away,
Wonderful words of life;

Glory, glory, glory,
Shout the wondrous story!

Chorus
Beautiful words, wonderful words,
Wonderful words of Life;
Beautiful words, wonderful words,
Wonderful words of Life.

12

SOME LIVE WORDS FOR TODAY'S CHURCH

When thou goest, it shall lead thee; when thou sleepest,
it shall keep thee; and when thou awakest, it shall talk with thee.
For the commandment is a lamp; and the law is light;
and reproofs of instruction are the way of life.

PROVERBS 6:22-23

Nobody would deny the power of words. In the Kingdom, we must be careful that the words before us are live words and that they are doing in us what they are intended to do. Despite the fact that many words have died in the house of their friends, there are live words imbued with power from on high. I want to give you some live words—words that are not zombies, not dead things, but living things for the hour.

Purgation

The first live word is "purgation." This word occurs in the Bible: "Purge me with hyssop, and I shall be clean: wash me, and I shall be whiter than snow" (Ps. 51:7). The meaning is that David desired to be purged from his old sins. The word "purgation" is a good word for our day.

What a difference it would be if a soldier on his way out to die was told, "Private Jones, have you been purged from your sins—are you clean by blood and fire?" I think you would get under that boy's skin with that question more than if you simply said, "Have you accepted Jesus?"

With the latter question, of course he will say, "I will," and bow his head and say, "I accept Jesus," and nothing comes of it. What a difference it would make to people if we go back to a living biblical word and say, "Jesus Christ came that He might cleanse people."

Today is the day of excusing sin instead of purging sin. An entire school of thought has developed around justifying sin within the Church and trying to prove that it is perfectly normal, and therefore, acceptable. Books are written to justify raising a little bit of hell while still being a good Christian. It is a terrible state of affairs, and we need to bring these fiery words back again.

Somebody will say that if you go around telling people they ought to be purged from sin, they will think you are crazy. You cannot do very much unless you are a little bit fanatical. If you insist upon being proper, you will be as sterile as a mule. That is our trouble today; we are sterile because we are proper.

The cults are fanatics, and their members are out winning rings around us. We would rather be proper and have people say about us, "He's a very well-balanced man; he has his head screwed on properly."

I do not want anybody to tell me I have my head screwed on. Nobody screwed the thing on. I do not care if they do say I am a fanatic, a radical. So was Paul, and so was Christ; so was

John Wesley, and so was A. B. Simpson. So is every man that has ever challenged his generation with ideas born of God and dared to throw off ideas that are dead—who has dared to throw off phrases that do not mean what they once meant and have lost their power.

People use phrases such as "separation" and "the regions beyond"—phrases that once embodied a living and breathing idea that motivated the entire church of Christ. Today they cease to live and breathe, and we are propagating and perpetuating the grave clothes of ideas that have died. Therefore, "purgation" is a word I recommend to you. Have you been purged from your sins?

Illumination

Another word I want to offer is "illumination." Nobody expects to be illuminated anymore. I believe, however, in inward illumination. If a man is purged from his sin, there will be an illumination inside him.

In history there were the Quakers who knew this illumination within. They had a light within. And the old Methodist and some others raised up a generation of people without much education or social graces. They picked their teeth with their penknife and threw the chicken bones to the dogs in the governor's palace, as Peter Cartwright did. They had come to the place where they received a sudden flash of illumination from above, and they knew the inward light.

The very fact that so many questions are being asked these days is a terrible indication that we are not being illuminated. The illuminated man does not ask questions, he answers them.

Today, everybody is asking questions; they will surround you and begin asking questions about this theological nicety and that hairsplitting, and what this theological shading means.

It was a generation of plowboys years ago, that stood up in their blue jeans and knew more theology than you can learn in any school. The man Isaiah said, "In the year that king Uzziah died I saw also the Lord sitting upon a throne, high and lifted up, and his train filled the temple" (Isa. 6:1). The man Ezekiel said, "Now it came to pass in the thirtieth year, in the fourth month, in the fifth day of the month, as I was among the captives by the river of Chebar, that the heavens were opened, and I saw visions of God" (Ezek. 1:1).

What we are languishing for in this day are a few men, just a few, that do not have to go and check with anybody to see if they are right. This is an illumination that nobody can know by nature. It is a flash from heaven that lights up the soul within.

At first, this man will be kicked all around; everybody will be afraid of him. He is too hot to handle. They will say, "Well, I'm afraid the poor fellow's in for trouble." He will flop around a while, and finally find himself and make everybody ashamed they thought he was a little off. We need illuminated people in these days. I believe in inward illumination.

Renunciation

I offer another word: "renunciation." Jesus said, "If any man will come after me, let him deny himself, and take up his cross, and follow me" (Matt. 16:24). We live in a day in which renunciation is no longer being taught. We are not supposed to renounce anything to become Christians. We are not told to, we are not supposed to. We just believe something and accept something passively, in moral inertia, and then go right back to what we were doing before. And there are men in this country who are making a career of compromising the cross of Christ with the world, until you cannot tell which is which. We are one big compromise.

When a man is converted, he ought to renounce his old life. We are members of a new creation, born from above, sons of the Father, joint heirs with the Son. Heaven is our home, hallelujah is our language, and we belong to a little company—a minority group despised and rejected of men.

Instead of that, Christianity has become popular. Evangelicalism has become popular and, consequently, it is dead. I once wrote a little essay called "Removing the Prayer Meetings—a Pagan Religion." I said, in effect, it is pagan praying when they pray and go right back to the set and make another picture.

Someone wrote me a very lovely, intelligent letter. He said, "I'm an evangelical. I am a graduate," and he named a certain fine Christian school, "Brother Tozer, your editorial sounded to me like evangelical prejudice against movies. Don't you think the time has come for us to rethink movies in the evangelical circles? There are some good movies, and we evangelical Christians ought not to go to the bad ones and raise the level of the movies. The thing sounds to me like categorical dogmatism."

I sat down and wrote him a letter: "Dear Brother, Your suggestion that we evangelicals accept the movies is old stuff. The modernist said that 30 years ago, and they rethought the movies with the results that they and the movies are like that now. And there's no separation."

Whenever you hear a man pleading for the right to be worldly, he is covering up a basic unbelief in his heart. The man who has been purged and illuminated will renounce the world, leave it and get out of it. If God converts a movie actress, we Christians have a right to demand that she get dressed, walk off the set and never go back. If God converts a gambler, we have a right to demand that he throw down his cards, walk out and pay everybody that he owes, if he can, and sell every horse and renounce the old bobtail nag.

But "renunciation" is a word we do not use anymore.

Immolation

Then I have another word for you: "immolation." That means offering yourself as a lamb on the altar. When the Old Testament priest took a lamb, put it on the altar, strapped it down and cut its throat—that was immolation. Paul said it in the twelfth chapter of Romans. Nowadays it is safety we are looking for instead of a place to die. God's people ought not to be looking for safety or a place to hide, but for a place to die, a place to give themselves as an offering to God.

God's people want to use Jesus as a lifeboat to get out of trouble. They want to use him as a bridge over the flame and then go back and live as they did before and never seek a place to immolate themselves.

Isn't it time somebody stopped looking for soft spots and cushions to fall on and places to hide? We who claim to be followers of the lowly Nazarene should begin to immolate ourselves and hunt an altar on which to die instead of look for an easy ride.

A few years ago, I had to settle something, and I settled it, I think, by the grace of God. I had to settle whether I was going to get old, peter out, get weak and preach in a high voice. Whether I would look for an easy life, make my bed, move off to a little lake with a cottage, play and live on my retirement. Or whether I was going to be a voice to this generation, come what may; whether I was going to hunt a place to die and ask God for the privilege of speaking God's Word to this generation.

Adoration

I have one more word: "adoration." You do not hear much about adoration anymore; we do not worship God anymore. I am a fanatic on the old hymns. But I am a fanatic with my eyes open, because I love to sing the things that adore my Maker. The music of the heart is adoration. The music of heaven is adoration. When we get to heaven, we will find that the harpers harping on their harps are just adoring God. They are not playing "Sweet Adeline" or "Huckleberry Hill." They are adoring God; and a Spirit-baptized man will be an adorer of God.

I do not want to go back and say what evangelicals were in the old days. That is old technique and I do not like it. I discovered the secret, if you can call it that, of their power in their generation. They loved Jesus until they shouted it out for joy. They adored the person of Jesus; they were harpers harping on their harps; some of their poetry was bad and they sang it off key, but they adored God.

I am looking for the fellowship of the burning heart. I claim the Methodist and the Baptist as mine, and I claim everybody that loves Jesus Christ as mine; but I am looking for the fellowship of the burning heart. Men and women of all generations and everywhere that love the Savior until "adoration" has become the new word, and they do not have to be entertained and amused. This Christ was everything, He was their all in all.

If we become worshipers of God, God will honor us in the hour in which we live. I think we ought to insist that we adore God and that we cannot adore Him until we are purged from our sins, illuminated by a fiery baptism, have renounced the world and all of its deceptions and then offer ourselves on an altar, ready to die. If we burn the bridge and give it all up, then there will be born in our hearts adoration—worship of the Lord Jesus Christ.

We sometimes sing Isaac Watts' old hymn with the lyrics, "I'll praise my Maker while I've breath, and when my voice is lost in death, praise shall employ my nobler powers."

The man, Isaac Watts, who wrote that in 1714, was an Englishman and a Calvinist. You say, "All right then, we've got to be a Calvinist in order to be adorers and worshipers." Let me tell you some more.

There was an Arminian by the name of John Wesley, an out-and-out Arminian. He did not believe any of this Calvinistic trash talk, as he called it. He said he believed in the Arminian theology. By the time he was 80 years old, he had traveled 25,000 miles on an old squeaky, bony horse's back, had established churches and set England ablaze. Now, as he is lying down, too weak to even sing anymore, he wants to die but he will not quit yet. He is waiting to go, and he is trying to sing in the meantime.

His friends around him bowed down real close to the old Arminian as he was dying, and they heard a little squeaky voice singing. When they got down low enough to hear what it was, what do you suppose it was? It was the old Calvinist song, "I'll praise my Maker while I've breath, and when my voice is lost in death, praise shall employ my nobler powers." Across the theological fence, Isaac Watts and John Wesley reached out and hugged each other tight and sang together.

I refuse to fight over theories, but I am looking for the fellowship of the burning heart. I am looking for men and women who are lost in worship, those who love God until He is the sweetheart of the soul.

Let us have the courage to stop using words that have lost their meaning. Do not just say "Amen" every time somebody gets up and shouts a phrase that we have been reared on. See whether it is dead or alive. Examine it a bit and say, "Wait a minute here now, is this thing living?" If it is alive, shout; and if it is not, bury it.

I thank God that I escaped from doctrinal hairsplitters and theological niceties. I thank God I was fanatical enough to shut my eyes and jump, and God took care of what is left.

Let us get some living ideas now. Let us preach again that men can be purged by fire and blood, that the Holy Spirit can illuminate within them and then they are called upon to renounce worldliness in every kind and offer themselves on an altar to die. Then if the result is not a fiery bush of adoration, I will miss my guess.

Let us be sincere about all this and you will find that our heavenly Father will come to us as in the ancient times, and we can know again the fiery flame and bring the burning bush back to religion.

I'll Praise My Maker While I've Breath

By Isaac Watts (1674-1748)

I'll praise my Maker while I've breath,
and when my voice is lost in death,
praise shall employ my nobler powers;
my days of praise shall ne'er be past,
while life, and thought, and being last,
or immortality endures.

Why should I make a man my trust?
Princes must die and turn to dust;
vain is the help of flesh and blood:
their breath departs, their pomp, and power,
and thoughts, all vanish in an hour,
nor can they make their promise good.

Happy the man whose hopes rely
on Israel's God: he made the sky,
and earth, and seas, with all their train;
his truth for ever stands secure,
he saves th'oppressed, he feeds the poor,
and none shall find his promise vain.

The Lord has eyes to give the blind;
the Lord supports the sinking mind;
he sends the lab'ring conscience peace;
he helps the stranger in distress,
the widow, and the fatherless,
and grants the pris'ner sweet release.

He loves his saints, he knows them well,
but turns the wicked down to hell;
thy God, O Zion! ever reigns:
Let every tongue, let every age,
in this exalted work engage;
praise him in everlasting strains.

I'll praise him while he lends me breath,
and when my voice is lost in death,
praise shall employ my nobler powers;
my days of praise shall ne'er be past,
while life, and thought, and being last,
or immortality endures.

13

GOD'S WAY IN HIS CHURCH

But Jesus answered them, My Father worketh hitherto, and I work.

JOHN 5:17

*For it is God which worketh in you both to will and
to do of his good pleasure.*

PHILIPPIANS 2:13

*Now there are diversities of gifts, but the same Spirit. And there
are differences of administrations, but the same Lord.*

1 CORINTHIANS 12:4-6

In considering how God works in His church, I want to acknowledge my indebtedness to Lady Julian of Norwich, a woman I met 600 years after she had stopped living and had gone to live in another, better world. Lady Julian's little book that I refer to quite often is called *The Revelations of Divine Love*. I will be using some quotes from that little book that will help explain God's way in His Church.

Allow me to lay this out in what I will call the five spiritual axioms that show how God works in His Church today. The comprehension of this will go a long way in understanding what God is doing not only in the Church universal but also in the individual Christian's life.

We Do Nothing of Ourselves

The first spiritual axiom I want to note is that *God does everything creative and constructive*. He does not do evil. Sin is a work of temporary rebellion against God, and the explanation is yet concealed. Sin is concealed; that is, the reason how the great God can be working and sin can still be in the world is concealed from us. We do not yet know because those concealed things are mystery.

People do not like the word "mystery," but it is a good Bible word, and it is a word we ought to learn to live with. For the world—everything round about us—is shrouded in mystery. Regarding things concealed, Lady Julian wrote, "And I saw not the creature doing, but I saw God doing in the creature."

Here is exactly what the Bible says both in the Old Testament and in the New Testament. Remember that when the Lord would work through Gideon, He did what some versions say as "clothed himself with Gideon" (Judg. 6:34). He took Gideon, put Gideon on and worked through Gideon and in Gideon did His mighty works. It was not Gideon doing it, but it was God working in the man Gideon.

Then we come to David and Goliath in the Old Testament, and we notice the upholding of this principle that God does everything that is constructive. God does it—not people or man or creature—but God. This is the reason there was no armor for David.

I do not suppose there would have been a committee or a board anywhere in Israel that would have gone along with David and allowed him to go out and meet the great overgrown Goliath, with his mighty sword as big as a weaver's beam, without armor. He could not have argued that idea to anybody. He could have argued, pleaded and written, but he could not have gotten anybody that would have allowed him to go out there without armor. And even David for a little bit put the armor of Saul on. But it was too big for him and he took it off and said it was not his armor. But if he had had to go through a committee or board to get this armor off, he never would have got it off. They would have sent him out there so loaded down with hardware that he could not have moved; and of course, Goliath would simply have pushed him over and tramped on him. But David did not go out that way; he had no armor.

Why did God send a man out without any armor against a giant who was covered with armor? Because God wanted to say, "God doth everything." He wanted to show that "it is God which worketh in you both to will and to do of his good pleasure" (Phil. 2:13). Why did He send David out against Goliath when there was such a vast disparity in size and strength? This man Goliath was a huge man, and David was an ordinary-sized man (I am not even sure that he was not a little undersized), and yet God pitted the two against each other. Why? It was that David might never boast about it anywhere. David never said to one of his wives, if she got a little out of hand, "Do you remember what I did to Goliath?" He knew he had not done it; God had done it.

Then there were the unequal weapons. The man David simply had five smooth stones, little marble-sized pebbles made round by rolling in the water. All he had was a slingshot. It was not a rubber slingshot such as boys use now; rubber had not been invented. Rather, it was made out of two strips of leather. Can you imagine God sending a young and undersized fellow out without any armor and without a proper weapon against a huge, oversized giant of a fellow who had proved his strength? Why, it is preposterous, but God did it because "it is God which worketh in you."

Notice the difficult passage in 1 Corinthians 12:4-6. God is telling how the Holy Spirit works in people and through people. God has a work to do, and He does it Himself in and through His people by the gifts of the Spirit. "Now there are diversities of gifts, but the same Spirit. And there are differences of administrations, but the same Lord. And there are diversities of operations, but it is the same God which worketh all in all." The point is that mortal minds cannot think immortal thoughts.

If we could only know that truth, there would be a lot of crawling at the church board meetings instead of coming with the assurance that we have the answers. There would be less answering of all the questions, and we would begin meekly to ask them. Mortal minds cannot think immortal thoughts. God has to think immortal thoughts through us or our thoughts are mortal thoughts, and mortal men cannot do immortal deeds. That is a total impossibility. God does His eternal works through the hands of men, yes, but it is the work of God in them.

Here is something most people do not know, and I suppose we will learn it and forget it, but God does not give us a reservoir of wisdom and power. If He did, it would very soon become stagnant. God never comes to a man according to the way we think about it, and pumps him full of wisdom and says, "If you get in any trouble, come see me or call me up, and pray; but in the meantime, you have a whole cistern full of power and wisdom here. You draw on that wisdom because it is yours." God never does it that way.

God does not give to a man a word of wisdom, and he does not give to a man power; but He is power in that man, and He is the word of wisdom in that man. It is God working in the man. It is not the man working. If we could only remember that. God becomes wisdom to us and He becomes power to us. That is why Christians blunder so.

If a man is a tall baseball player, 12 years in the big league, we say, "He's skillful, he has learned. He's got experience." It is the same with anything people do. They learn by experience, they learn how to do things by doing them. But in the kingdom of God, it is completely other than that. A man can be 75 years old and have served God most of his lifetime and yet make a critical blunder and be so ignorant and uncouth, because God is not working through the man or in the man. The man himself is right back where he was when he started. I say it again: It is God that worketh in you.

God did not send me out to be a marriage counselor; He sent me out to preach the gospel; and if He gives me a word for somebody, it is His Word, and it will help people. But if I think that I, out of years of experience, can tell people how they ought to live, I am only making a fool out of myself. And there is a great deal of this kind of fool-making going on in the church of Christ in the name of Christianity. We forget that we have no wisdom for anybody unless God wants to give us the wisdom at the moment. Jesus said, "But when they deliver you up, take no thought how or what ye shall speak: for it shall be given you in that same hour what ye shall speak" (Matt. 10:19).

Every created thing, every eternal thing—it is God who does it. It is God who is doing it. Man is not doing it. If God were to strip the churches from all that man is doing and leave only what He has done or is doing, we would trim the average church back down to a nubbin. There would not be enough left to have a decent service. But all of the churches are running on their own steam; they have learned how. They have gone to school to find out how, and have written books on pastoral psychology and pastoral theology—"How to Do It in 10 Easy Lessons." The answer and the result is that we just do not know. We count on our reservoir in place of our Lord.

If you talk to a Christian Scientist or a Roman Catholic on Wednesday, and you have an amazing success with them and even maybe win one of them to Christ, and then on Friday you try the same way, you could fall flat on your face. Because God is working in you on Wednesday, but on Friday you were looking to what God did on Wednesday, expecting Him to work that same way on Friday. He may even write a book about it. I have seen books on how to win Roman Catholics and what to say to Christian Scientists and how to answer Jehovah's Witnesses. You can answer one on Monday, answer successfully, and try it on Wednesday and he will put a half nelson on you and throw you to the mat. It takes the Holy Spirit to work in a man. Always keep that in mind.

God does everything, and man does nothing. It is only God that is working. Remember, it is the eternal Lord who is creating a new generation and a new creation. Just as Adam did not create himself, and just as the angels did not create themselves but God created them, so He is building His Church. People are not building the Church. God is building the Church. If He were not building His Church, all you would have is simply a religious organization.

God Foresees All That He Does

The second spiritual axiom is that God *does all in His foreseeing wisdom*. All that God is doing and has done, He is doing in His foreseen wisdom; so nothing is done by happenstance or by venture. Everything God does He does in His foreseen wisdom. God knows our tomorrows, He knows our day after tomorrow, He knows all about us down the years and it has all been planned before our time was.

All that is now happening is within the wisdom of God established before any star was ever created. Long before there was matter, motion or law, God had foreseen it all. Either you believe that or you will be frustrated and miserable all the time. The Bible teaches that God does it all in His foreseen wisdom. He foresaw it all, and He is not allowing anything to happen. The world is not a truck running downhill with the driver having a heart attack at the wheel. No, the world is moving toward a pre-determined end, and God Almighty, who is standing in the shadows, is seeing it go, watching it and guiding it.

The nation of Israel and the nations of the world and Christendom, and the true Church that He hides in His own heart—God knows where they all are, at all times, by his infinite and perfect wisdom. He is running everything according to plans He made before Adam ever stood up on the earth. Before there was Abraham or David or Isaiah or Paul, before Jesus was born in Bethlehem's manger, God had this all planned.

Do not think of God sitting down with a pencil and working it out the way you and I would have to do it. God thinks, and it is done. He wills, and it comes to pass. God does not have to work with a pencil, a slide rule, a compass and a square the way architects and builders do. "In the beginning was the Word, and the Word was with God, and the Word was God. The same was in the beginning with God. All things were made by him; and without him was not any thing made that was made" (John 1:1-3). How was that? He was the Word, and He spoke and it was done.

When Jacob fled from the face of his angry brother and was in the howling wilderness, he saw a ladder standing up on the earth. I still wonder whether Jacob would ever have seen that ladder if he had not been on the run. Had Jacob been back home in good company, staying around the house, helping his mother with the dishes, he never would have encountered the ladder.

I would like to suggest that sin is always wrong, and when we rebel against God, we are going to get ourselves into real serious trouble. But remember another thing, that if you are God's, you belong to Him. And if you have learned the art of true repentance, God will turn even your defeat into a victory. Fleeing Jacob saw a ladder.

Saul was breathing out and threatening slaughter, and suddenly he stands and sees Stephen die. Undeterred, he goes away from there; and on his way, on the road to Damascus, he sees the Lord high and lifted up, and he hears a voice and is a converted man. I wonder if Saul would have ever been converted had he been a quiet professor in Gamaliel's university and had simply said, "Well, there is no use to get excited about it, no use to get excited. Everything will work out all right." If he had said that, there would never have been a Paul—that mighty servant of God. But Saul was a man, the root of the matter was in him, and so God observed the man's wrongdoing, turned him around, started him right and then began to work in his life.

God Works Above Our Understanding

The third spiritual axiom is that *much that God is doing looks to us like an accident or a mistake.* Due to our blindness and our ignorance, we do not know why God is doing what He is doing, and so we begin to fidget and wonder if God does really know. However, God sees tomorrow; we see only today. God sees both sides; we see only one side. God knows that we do not know and God has all the pieces to the puzzle; you and I have only a few of the pieces.

Here is our pattern of life, and we like to see it bloom into a beautiful picture where everything is in place; but it has all scattered around and we do not know where the pieces are; nothing fits. Did you ever take a puzzle and do this? Did you ever take two pieces that look as if they belong together and try to force them in place? And then you broke an edge off and are worse off than you were before?

But we take the work of God and we try to push pieces together. I think a good part of my life has been trying to shove together pieces that do not go together, and trying to separate pieces that do. This is ignorance. We forget that it is God that gives us the wisdom. It is God that works in us, if only we would let God do His work in us. That is why I believe in the gifts of the Spirit. I do not think I have done myself any good with the evangelical hierarchy by coming out as I have on the gifts; I always have believed that all gifts of the Spirit ought to be in the Church today the same as they were back at Pentecost.

God is working through His people, and what God works lasts. What God does not work will not last; and I do not care how much personality a man has, he cannot do immortal work, because he is a mortal man. He cannot think immortal thoughts, because he has a mortal mind. But if the Holy Ghost works in him and through him, He giveth to every man severally as He will. And it is the same Father working in us and through us.

Those "accidents" that you and I think we are in are not accidents at all. If a man follows the Lord, he will not find any accidents. He will find God working his life out for him.

If you trust God, He will bring you out of all that. It will not be an accident. The accidents I thought were accidents were simply God helping me through when I did not know He was doing it.

God Never Changes

Another spiritual axiom that I borrow from Lady Julian is that *God changes never, He is perfect.* "No, never shall He, world without end." God never changes His purpose nor ever shall, world without end. That does not sound to me as if it had been given 600 years ago, but it was. But, it's part of truth; the Word of God, the gifts and callings of God, are without repentance.

God never loses heart. I would like to have you know that. Religious people lose heart. I have seen some good, godly people turn into an emotional spin and become so low that there was no describing how low they were. But God never gets low, because He sees the end from the beginning. To God these things have already happened. If you knew you had to die tomorrow, you would feel a little low tonight, for a while, and then you would get elated. But God never rises, never gets up and then down and up and then down, because everything has already happened with God. And God is not going around watching dials and looking at gauges, seeing if everything is all right and testing to see if you are on the beat. No, God does not have to do that. God changeth never His purpose, no, never shall, world without end. He is moving toward a purpose in Christ Jesus before the world began.

When the angels sang over Bethlehem's manger, they were not announcing anything new. It had been known all the way back to the Garden of Eden, and it had been known to the heart of God before there was Eden, or an Adam or an Eve. So God changes His mind never; no, never shall be.

God said to Jonah, "Go and preach in Nineveh." Jonah bought a ticket in another direction. God changes not His mind, no, He never shall. Therefore, Jonah ended up preaching in Nineveh.

Conditions and things may seem helpless. A man asked me one time why God did not condense the Bible, all that old, dry history. You know what that old, dry history teaches? That God is working providentially through men. That history is the footprints of God, the footprints of God of history. The way that God worked with Abel, Noah, Abraham, Lot and all the rest, down to us, that is why we have heard of these men so

much, because it is the way God works. And He has not changed
His mind.

God Never Abandons What He Has Begun

The last spiritual axiom is, *God never lifts His hands off His work.*
He leads all things to an ordained end. He never lifts His hands
off His work. When Michelangelo died, he had a backyard
stacked full of partly completed statues. Michelangelo was an
Italian, and in addition to having the high, hot Latin temperament, he had a double charge of genius worth five crowns.

That was Michelangelo. He saw a piece of rock and was not
willing to wait around to finish it. And so he had a whole backyard full of statues that he had started but lost heart and did
not finish. He had done an amazing amount of work, but there
was an amazing amount of work he was too impatient to finish. If we could give him another day, the statues might have
turned into what he wanted. Instead of that, he threw them out
in the backyard—half-done pieces of art.

God never lifts His hands off His work; no, never. I believe
that. I do not care what happens, I believe it. God never lifts His
hands off His work; when God says, "You do this," it means,
"You go do it, and I will work through you, and I will not be discouraged; you may be discouraged, but I will not."

There is an old saying, "The higher up a monkey goes, the
more his tail shows," and the devil rises up there. If the devil
only knew that if you hit God's people hard enough, they will
brace themselves. All you have to do is to get after God's people
just enough and you bring out everything that is in them.
When everything is going all right with me, I am one of the lazi-

est, easygoing persons you ever saw in your life. But when things fight against me, I back up a few steps and suddenly say, "Hold on here," and the very intention of the devil that wants to drive me back has the opposite effect.

I believe it is true of Christians everywhere. God does not take His hand off His work; He is moving toward a preordained plan; and if we work with Him in that plan, Satan's efforts to stop us can only cause us to snap our teeth sharp and say in the name of God and in the strength of Jehovah, we are going forth.

God never takes His hand off His work but has declared a preordained end by the same wisdom of power and love by which He created everything in the first place. You are no accident; do not think you are. God made all things by preordained purpose, by foreknowledge; and when you came into the Kingdom, you were not an accident.

Back to the beginning when there was nothing, God knew all about that and knew what things He would bring with Him when He came. Knew when He would come, knew what He would say. God never lifts His hand off His work. He does it by wisdom, power and love. There is no less wisdom, no less power, no less love now than ever was.

This is hard for us to understand because we cannot see it. We must just believe. Believing is a kind of seeing. But we are not seeing down on our human level. The human level gets us in trouble.

Years ago, I heard a man preach a sermon. He said, "The Christian has three men inside of him. The old man, the new man and the you-man. That is all there is until he is converted, and then he gets the new man." I liked that. There is a human nature, and the human nature gets in so much trouble. Even long after victory has been won over the old man, the new man just gets you down. That is the part that gets blue and the part that gets arrogant over things and gets carnal about things. The old man must die in order to live in the power of the new man, and new man keeps the human sort of under control.

God does everything in His foreseen wisdom. While much that He does looks like an accident to you and to me because we do not know enough, God never changes His plans, never will, and never lifts His hand off His work, but goes forward toward His preordained purpose, using even people like you and me.

Arise, My Soul, Arise!
By Charles Wesley (1707-1788)

Arise, my soul arise;
Shake off thy guilty fears;
The bleeding Sacrifice
In my behalf appears.
Before the throne my Surety stands,
Before the throne my Surely stands,
My name is written on His hands.

He ever lives above,
For me to intercede;
His all redeeming love,
His precious blood, to plead.
His blood atoned for all our race,

His blood atoned for all our race,
And sprinkles now the throne of grace.

Five bleeding wounds He bears,
Received on Calvary;
They pour effectual prayers;
They strongly plead for me.
"Forgive him, oh, forgive," they cry,
"Forgive him, oh, forgive," they cry,
"Nor let that ransomed sinner die!"

The Father hears Him pray,
His dear Anointed One;
He cannot turn away,
The presence of His Son.
His Spirit answers to the Blood,
His Spirit answers to the Blood,
And tells me I am born of God.

My God is reconciled;
His pard'ning voice I hear.
He owns me for His child;
I can no longer fear.
With confidence I now draw nigh,
With confidence I now draw nigh,
And, "Father, Abba, Father," cry.

14

THE MINISTRY OF THE NIGHT

The day is thine, the night also is thine: thou hast prepared the light and the sun.

PSALM 74:16

Occasionally, an uninspired poet will say something nice about the night such as, "How beautiful is night! A dewy freshness fills the silent air" (Robert Southey 1774–1843). But our instinct is away from the night and toward the day. I am talking about the physical night and day, because we are made for the day; we are not nocturnal creatures, we are diurnal. We belong to the day. And in the sacred Scriptures, much is made of the idea of day and night. The day symbolizes the kingdom of God, heaven, righteousness and everlasting peace; and the night symbolizes the reign of sin, destruction and hell at last.

Light in Nature

The purest of the non-inspired concepts about God that I have known or ever heard about is that of the Parsees, a Zoroastrian community in India. They felt after God, if perchance they might find Him, and they came up with the doctrine we now know as fire worship of the Parsee or Zoroastrians. Their belief is that God is the light, therefore they worship the sun and they keep fire burning on their altars continually.

And in the light of the day, we have a number of things we cannot have in pitch-darkness. For instance, we have knowledge. A man who stands in pitch-darkness may be standing within one foot of a cliff over which he might easily stumble to his death, or he might be standing within one foot of his own door and not know it, because it takes light to bring knowledge.

Then there is a perception of the relation of one thing to another that comes in the light that cannot possibly be present in the day. Because man is a traveler on his way, somewhere there has to be light. Not even the compass will lead if you do not have the light to see the compass. There must be light, because we are travelers and we must go; and as the sun is the lord of the day, giving knowledge, perception and information, so God is the Lord of the kingdom of light. He is the Lord of the kingdom of holiness, justice, wisdom, love and peace.

Light in Morality

The apostle John says, "God is light" (1 John 1:5); and God calls us into the light. I'm thinking about this morally now, and I would say that the simplest and most elementary description of conversion would be that God calls a man from dishonesty into honesty; from moral wickedness into purity; from hate to love; from envy to charity; from lying to truth; from evil to good; and this I say is elementary, and certainly not enough. It does not explain enough, but that is true, nevertheless. And this call of God from the darkness of wickedness to the light of truth and holiness is a constant call, always being heard. When the dweller in darkness comes into the light, what a radiance of beauty he sees for the first time! What a lifting of the load is this, and what a rolling away of fear, and what an inward well of comfort there springs up, and a seeing of the Son. That is conversion!

I sometimes think that after we have been Christians for a long while, we tend to forget what happened when we were first converted. We begin to take ourselves for granted, as a couple that has been married a few years or so will do. The radiance of the first day in the new home fades away and they begin to take each other for granted. I think every once in a while we Christians ought to, just for the sake of giving our own souls a refresher, go over our conversion again and see what did happen at conversion.

The Scripture says that the day belongs to God, and it is talking about the moral part of things—the light, the holiness, the morality, the purity, the joy—that all belong to God; but it also says the night belongs to God. And here we come to a different meaning of the word, because the word that we see here is an extension, borrowed from the old world.

Just as Israel, down in Egypt, had the night all around about them, and the night was God's night and belonged to God; they had light in their dwelling. Many of God's children cannot stand the light of the night.

I must explain again that by the night, I do not mean wickedness. I mean that state of affairs, which wickedness has brought to the world, which we must live in the midst of but of which we are not a part of. All the evil that is in the world is here; it is darkness, and we must remember that the sovereign God holds that in His hands. If there were any part of God's world that He did not have control over, there would soon be a rebellion that would shake the throne on high. But God is the sovereign God, and the night also is His; and though He has no affinity with the wickedness of the world, He is in control of the world. And the darkness that comes around us is also in His hand, and we are in His hand.

There are those of God's children who cannot learn this. They fear the night and they whither in the darkness. They are children only of the day, and they have never learned the ministry of the dark night of the soul. God has to leave a light on for them as we sometimes leave a light on for a frightened child until it goes to sleep. God has to keep some people out of trouble because they are not strong enough spiritually ever to know how to deal with trouble; and if they do not have trouble, they will not have growth. And so there is the vicious circle. God cannot expose them to the night and yet they cannot grow until they have had the cooling dews of the night.

Others learn to walk in darkness. They are not walking in moral darkness but are living in a dark world, as Peter said that we are living in the darkness holding forth the word of truth (see 1 Pet. 2:9-12).

Now, we are thinking of the better aspects of the night not as the moral evil but the inconveniences and the hindrances and tribulations that result from living in a world of night. The sovereign God forces even the darkness to serve His will and compels the sullen night to discipline His children. You and I never want it to rain. We want the sun to shine continually; but if the sun shone continually, the earth would be baked so hard you could not sink a pick into it. It takes the cool rain mingled with the warm sun to produce the vegetation and to bless the flora and the fauna that God has given us to enjoy.

In 2 Corinthians, there is a passage very dear to my heart. It says this: "For our light affliction, which is but for a moment, worketh for us a far more exceeding and eternal weight of glory" (2 Cor. 4:17). I want you to see the sharp contrast here. There is affliction, but it is light; there is glory, but it is heavy. There is affliction, but it is for a moment; there is glory, but it is eternal; and if we keep this in mind, we would not be afraid of the night and we would not always have to have God put a light on to keep us from whimpering.

Momentary Light Affliction

The night has a ministry to you and me. By the night, I mean these circumstances in a fallen world. The situation we are in now—occasional visitation of sickness, the loss of a loved one, the failure of our hopes and the disappointment we have when people fail us, and all of these things. Along with this, there are the attacks of the enemy and of the devil himself coming to us. All of these are, in a sense, darkness at work; we are in the midst of it and we cannot escape it. The Scriptures teach this, and the hymns that we sing so often teach this as well.

I am quite astonished how we sing one way and believe another. I think we ought to go over our hymns, and the ones we have determined not to believe we should throw out and save ink and trouble. But if they are true, we ought to hold them to be true and if they are not we ought to say so. God loves candid people, and He has very little to do with conventional things merely for convention's sake.

So if it is not so that there is joy that the Cross is a beautiful thing to carry and that joy cometh in the morning after a night of weeping; if it is not true, then we ought to quit quoting it. If it is true, we ought to start believing it.

God discovers occasionally a soul that He can trust. He lets the mysterious signs come to them, the mysterious evidences that they have been chosen out of Him. His hand is laid on their shoulder, and He has marked them as being different. They are going to be great Christians, great souls. Let us not think for a moment that all people are alike in the world. They are certainly not all alike in the kingdom of Adam. There are ignorant men, educated men, great men, simple men, small men and large men. There are people with many talents and people with few, and a few with none. They are not alike in this world and they are not going to be alike in the Kingdom of Light either. Some men in the Kingdom of Light are slated for greatness in God's kingdom, and some will simply be there, I suppose, to sit on the golden chair and fill up the heavens. I do not know what else they are for.

I have known many of the Lord's people; they are going to go to heaven by the grace of God, but they have never been much use here and they probably will not be much account there unless the Lord has a new way of doing things that He has not revealed in the sacred Scriptures. But there are some that the Lord has laid His hand on, and they are going to be great in God. I do not mean famous, I mean great in God; they're going to be rich beyond all the dreams of avarice, and God is employing every means to make them spiritually great. He is using the day with its sun and the night with its darkness. He is using good people with their hope and cheer and He is using bad people with their persecution. He is using help with its bounty and perhaps illness.

I would rather believe the Bible than believe what I find in a book somewhere. In the Bible, I find the man got sick and when he got sick, he turned unto the Lord. He said, "Before I was afflicted I went astray: but now have I kept thy word" (Ps. 119:67). The churches believed through the centuries that the Lord sometimes chastens His people by letting illness happen to them. You will find that in 1 Corinthians 11:27-34, and you will find much else in the Scriptures that would teach the same thing. So every time you get a pain, do not accept the modern silly idea that that pain is the result of your failing the Lord somewhere. The Lord may turn that pain into glory.

When God Almighty turns loose on us the ministry of day and night, of good and bad, of God and the devil, He makes the devil work for us. He harnesses him like the dumb donkey that he is and makes him pull the cart for the saints of God. God has always done it and He is still doing it. When the devil starts out roaring to seek whom he may devour, God bottles up his roar and makes it work for the Kingdom and for the saints of the most high God. Winds that blow and the stars in their courses fight for the men and women God delights to honor.

God of Night as Well as Light

The ministry of the night is that heartache you have carried around with you and are carrying now, the night of suffering.

Job had not only bodily pain but also had the worst pain of suspicion and blame. His own wife turned on him and sarcastically told him that he ought to give up. He said to her, "What? Shall we receive good at the hand of God, and shall we not receive evil?" (Job 2:10).

Job's wife disappeared, and she was never heard of again. But Job did have to endure a lot of it. God allowed three eloquent friends of his that had eaten at his table to come and start spouting poetry to prove that Job had been a hypocrite all the time. Now, if you think that is easy to take, try it sometime. Job had it to do. It was a long time and Job said, "But he knoweth the way that I take: when he hath tried me, I shall come forth as gold" (Job 23:10).

Jesus was called the man of sorrow. That is why I cannot think that we happified Christians who always want to giggle, that we are true followers of the man of sorrow. Because He was a man of sorrows, and acquainted with grief. Those who follow Christ will have many nights of sorrow.

I think of our old friend Abraham, who took the knife to slay his only son (see Gen. 22:1-19). God grabbed his wrist quick enough to stop it. But all the psychological inward pain of it had already taken place when he said yes to God, "I will slay my son." Already he had died inside of his heart. Already he was a wounded man slowly bleeding to death. God staunched the wound, healed him and gave him back his son. Gave him back everything else, blessed him and made his name great. Then all the nations of the earth have been blessed through him. But Abraham had to know the sudden settling down of the dark night in the midst of day. He had to know it.

I think of the prophet Jeremiah. I find many men who are wandering around that are not any good, and many men who are the messengers and saints of God who are not wanted. You cannot always tell whether God is blessing a man by how many calls he gets, because many men get calls that if the truth were known about them, they would never be called anywhere, except to a court of law. Other men are God's own saints but are not wanted.

I remember an old Irish preacher by the name of Robert J. Cunningham, a dear old friend of mine. He always said he was between 25 and 80, which is all he would tell me. And I never knew how old he was. He was one of those men so thin he could not get any thinner, and so dry that even his breath did not have any moisture in it; but he was a saint. He would look up at the ceiling and preach to his congregation. They criticized him for praying too much. He said one time, "If the only criticism my friends have against me is that I pray too much, why it's all right; it's not too bad." He was something of a failure. Nobody called him and said, "Brother Cunningham, come and preach to 500 ministers." Nobody ever said that to him, because he would come and stand up there and look at the ceiling and talk in a dry way. But God was on that man. He was a saint; he walked with God "and was not," for God took him.

Failure sometimes is an evidence of the hand of God upon you, and we Christians can afford to fail because Jesus afforded to fail. He died out there on the cross, and it looked as if it was a battered tragic stupid end of a man who meant well but did not know how to handle Himself. On the third day, God raised Him from the dead and set Him at His own right hand and made Him to be head over all things to the Church and put all things under His feet, whether they be principalities, powers, or dominions, all are under His feet (see Eph. 1:19-23), and yet He died an apparent failure. Only "apparently," for He was a roaring success before the world was created, and in this hour, and will be in all the worlds to come. Failure sometimes is night.

What did people think of John the Baptist? They said he had better never been born. What a failure, what a hopeless wretch he was. I heard somebody say when John the Baptist died that somebody on earth said, "Oh, John the Baptist is dead," and somebody in heaven said, "Oh, here comes John the Baptist." It's all in the way you look at it.

Night of Coldness

I wrote a little editorial called "How to Keep From Going Stale." I believe this staleness comes to all the Lord's children. It comes sometimes even to the best of His children; they get rather dull and cold. David had those spells, and he blamed them on God. He went to God and said, "God you did it, and now bless me and bring me out of this." He did not go off somewhere and try to blame it on his wife, but said, "Oh, God, you've turned away from me; bless me now," and the Lord heard his prayer and restored him again to warmth.

Do you ever have those cold periods that you cannot seem to do anything with? Some of you have never had warms periods long enough to know the difference. A man who has never been warm will never find it out when he gets cold. But those of you who have had your long warm spell, there have also been times that have been cold spells.

I've gotten up many a morning when, if I went on my feelings, I would have laid back down, literally, and not only laid back down but also flattened out and given up and quit planning ever to get up. But you do not work and you do not live according to your feelings. When the time comes for you to pay your taxes, you don't pay them only if you feel good, and not pay them if you feel bad. You pay them, period. When it comes time for you to go to work, you do not say to your wife, "I'm feeling low this morning." You get up and go to work. We walk by faith. We do what we have to do and know we ought to do, and we pay no attention to our coldness or warmness. I admit it is nice to be warm. We can read in the Psalms many times when David had his cold spells. They were the ministry of the night.

Isaiah said that he was undone, a man of unclean lips (see Isa. 6:5). We walk by faith; and often a glimpse into our own hearts will so disconcert us and grieve us that we can have no present joy. I find it possible to walk around without any joy. I find it possible to live in the heart of God without any joy for a little while. By these means—suffering and sorrow, loss, failure, cold spells, penitence and tribulation—God makes that which is outward inward. And He perfects the Garden eastward in the soul of each of His children.

In *Revelations of Divine Love,* Lady Julian of Norwich said this: "For the tender love that our good Lord hath to all that shall be saved, He comforteth readily and sweetly, signifying thus: It is sooth that sin is cause of all this pain; but all shall be well, and all shall be well, and all manner [of] thing shall be well." The sooner we learn to appreciate the ministry of the night, the sooner we will lose all apprehensions associated with the night.

All Must Be Well

By Mary Bowley Peters (1813-1856)

Through the love of God our Savior, All will be well;
Free and changeless is His favor, All, all is well.
Precious is the blood that healed us,
Perfect is the grace that sealed us,
Strong the hand stretched forth to shield us,
All must be well

Though we pass through tribulation, All will be well.
Ours is such a full salvation, All, all is well.
Happy still in God confiding;
Fruitful if in Christ abiding;
Steadfast through the Spirit's guiding:
All must be well

We expect a bright tomorrow; All will be well.
Faith can sing through days of sorrow, All, all is well
On our Father's love relying,
Jesus every need supplying;
Or in living or in dying
All must be well

15

How to Know When a Thing Is from God

Prove all things; hold fast that which is good.

1 Thessalonians 5:21

Beloved, believe not every spirit, but try the spirits whether they are of God: because many false prophets are gone out into the world.

1 John 4:1

I want to share a little spiritual treasure God gave me some years back to tell if a doctrine is from Him or not; whether a blessing I am receiving or an emotional experience I may have or a miracle I may think I see, or anything else, is of God. Some Christians, of course, cannot profit by this for the simple reason that they are static. They have had no new experiences, and they are not going to have any, if they can help it. They are satisfied to beat their wings fast and buzz around low. But you that are seekers after God, you that are troubled and concerned about your spiritual lives, this is for you.

Some people are troubled in their spiritual lives. They read the Bible, but that does not help them. They do not seem to be able to find themselves. They are ready to hear from anyone, and that is a danger. I do not like to see anybody too willing to accept things. I like to have them do what the Bereans did—examine the Scriptures to see if these things are true (see Acts 17:11).

Some people are eager and seeking some new thing. You hear everybody and his brother lecturing, talking and giving messages. It's all right; radio is a good medium of communication. But you have to use your head and your heart. Just the fact that he talks fast and sounds pious does not mean one thing. The devil can come as an angel of light. So you have to learn to know an angel of light from an angel of God. You have to learn to know pseudo truth from truth.

There are those who are willing to take up a new doctrine and seek new experiences if somebody else comes along and demonstrates they have had one. And there are always those who are easily moved by miracles. I have never been. I have seen God do some miracles, but I have never been much convinced by miracles. If they will not believe Moses, the prophets, the apostles and our Lord, they would not believe even if a man rose from the dead. Miracles are secondary proofs of anything, and yet miracles move some people tremendously; and if somebody can come along and do a miracle, they would just believe anything.

I want to give you a rule to help along this line: The rule is to check "the new thing" by asking how does it affect my attitude toward and my relation to God, Christ, the Scriptures, myself, other Christians, the world and sin?

Attitude Toward God

Suppose you hear a new doctrine that has come your way by some fellow who perspires and talks sumptuously. All right now, he has got his doctrine, but *what does that doctrine do for God?* Does it make God great or small? Does it make God necessary or less necessary? Does it put God where He belongs— does it bring glory to Him and humble me and show me how little I am and how great God is? Or does it obscure God and draw a veil across the face of God?

Whatever makes God less important or less wonderful or less glorious or less mighty is not of God. The whole purpose of God in redemption and for sending the Scriptures and redeeming man is that He might be glorified among men. The glory of God is the health of the universe. Wherever God is not glorified, that part of the universe is sick.

Hell is sick because God is not glorified there. Heaven is abounding in glorious health because God is glorified there. Earth is halfway in-between sick and well, because only some glorify God, and the rest do not. The glory of God is the health of the universe; and the sound of the anthems of praise to God Almighty is the music of the spheres. Therefore, any doctrine, any phase or emphasis of doctrine; any experience that I may seem to have; any miracle that I may seem to have seen; if it does not make God big and keep Him big and make God indispensable and wonderful, then put it away and say, "I'll have nothing to do with anything that diminishes God."

Attitude Toward Christ

How does this new thing affect our *attitude toward and our relation to Christ?* Because Christ is who He is and what He is, He is indispensable. He is and always will be necessary to the point where we must have Him. Any teaching, any experience, any fellowship, any activity that makes Christ less necessary to us cannot be of God.

Say that you have gone to the altar. You have prayed, you have been blessed, you have heard teachings given by men with breath in their nostrils. The fact that Dr. So-and-so said it does not make it true. The fact that I have said it does not make it true. The fact that your Bible teachers said it does not make it true. We can be mistaken. You have to test us, as well as everybody else, and search the Scriptures.

Has our teaching made Christ bigger, grander, sweeter and more indispensably beautiful now than He was before? If He is, you have every good reason to believe that you have been hearing from God. If He is less glorious, and you have become attached to man, then the teaching you have had is bad or at least it has been given in a bad way. Jesus Christ is absolutely necessary. He is the divine imperative. He is the one without whom we cannot live. We must have Him and we must be in Him and He in us. If it is of God, your dependence on God and your dependence on Christ will increase, and Christ will become sweeter and more wonderful all the time.

I do not say He will become sweeter as the years go by. We sing that song, but I do not believe it half the time I hear it. The same old deacon who sings "Sweeter as the Years Go By" every second Sunday morning for 20 years is the same sour, sulky, stubborn old person he was before, only he is a little older, that is all. Let us not sing it if we do not mean it. I would rather sit quietly and never croak an "amen," than to lie to God and the people. But if He is more glorious every day, it is no harm in saying so; and I believe in coming out and saying so.

Jesus Christ, our Lord, is indispensable; He is above all; and any experience, any interpretation of Scripture that does not make Him big and great and wonderful, is not of God. For God wants to make His Son glorious, and the Son wants to make the Father glorious, and the Holy Spirit wants to make the Father and the Son glorious. And so anything that comes to you, even an archangel with a wingspread of 40 feet and shining like a neon sign were to come down here and tell me that he has just seen a miracle and wants me to come, I would want chapter and verse. I would want to know that he was from God. I am not running after any will-o'-the-wisp.

I bother many people. They wonder why I am not all worked up about them when they come steaming in. I am not going to be worked up over a man with his breath in his nostrils. Here is my book—the Bible; here are my two knees, and I am still able to bend them. When I get so old and rheumatic that I can't bend them, I can stand up and pray. God Almighty hears His people pray, and I have a line open to Him. When people tell me the Lord told them to tell me something, I say, "My line is open to God; why didn't He tell me?" I reject it unless it obviously makes God wonderful and makes Jesus Christ beautiful; then I'll give it an ear. But that doesn't happen very often.

Attitude Toward the Scriptures

How does this new experience, this new interpretation, this new preacher or new emphasis affect *our attitude toward and our relationship to the Scriptures?* Are they more or less precious to us?

A woman once came to me and said, "Mr. Tozer, I'd like to ask you a question. I'm troubled."

I said, "What is your trouble?"

She told me, "Our pastor has gone forward in the things of God, and he's gone so fast that he tells us God's given him new revelations that are not in the Scriptures. And he wants us to divest our minds of all that we've learned and follow him, and he says that we'll be sinning if we don't follow him."

I told her in a nice, scholarly way to tell him to go get lost and for her to go back to the Word of God. No man will ever be able to persuade me to follow him unless he follows the Scriptures. Here is the Book; here is the Book to the law and to the testimony. If they speak not according to the law, it's because there is no truth in them. He that hath the dream let him tell the dream; but he that hath the Word let him speak My Word faithfully. You can always check with the Word.

If this new experience does not make you read the Word more, it is not of God. If it does not make you meditate on the truth more, it is not of God. And I do not care how good you feel. If you feel so good you feel brand new, as the camp meeting song used to have it, you are still not being blessed of God.

Some might ask, "Is it possible to have an emotional experience that is not of God?" I should say so. It is entirely possible to get emotional experiences that are not of God. But I believe that true experiences carry an emotional overtone, and for that reason, I have no objection whatever to emotions. I believe the Lord's people ought to be the happiest and most radiant people in the world, and I believe they ought not to hesitate to speak right out and say "amen" when they feel like it. If it is not just a habit, it is just so much dry wood. So ask yourself, how do these experiences affect my attitude toward the Scriptures?

Attitude Toward Myself

Then, how does this new thing affect *our attitude toward ourselves?* Whatever comes from God diminishes self and glorifies God. Whatever comes from God humbles us. Whatever comes from God makes the flesh intolerable. But if it comes from the flesh, it puffs up and makes us feel superior; it makes us look down on other Christians.

Did you ever meet Christians with their noses elevated at a 45-degree angle from the level field? They smile down from their imperial heights and say, "You do not understand me, just pray about it," and they go away looking like Saint Frances. But all they had was a bad case of pride. It was just pride grown bad, grown cancerous. No, whatever is of God always humbles you. If it is of God, it makes you appreciate your fellow Christians that much more. And it makes you appreciate the humblest, poorest Christian in the whole congregation and makes you love that Christian.

Self puffs up, makes you look down on other people and makes you pity them and smile down on them. Never put yourself on a pedestal. In you dwelleth no good thing. I do not care who you are or how many degrees you have or anything that you might say or have justly said about you. Any experience that is of God, any doctrine that is of God, humbles my flesh and brings me down lowly before Him; it makes Him great and me little.

Attitude Toward Other Christians

How do these experiences or these new doctrines or emphases *affect our relationship with other Christians?* Are other Christians more dear to us or less dear to us? Are we drawn to them or not?

Whatever brings separation in spirit from others of God's children cannot possibly be of God.

Now, you would say you do not believe in separation. Yes, I do believe in separation. If your pastor is teaching that the Bible is not the Word of God, that Christ is not the Son of God, that the Scriptures are not to be trusted, that they are only partly true, that the new birth is an old-fashioned idea, that the blood of Christ does not cleanse, then I say the thing for you to do is separate yourself. I would not give one dime to support a lazy preacher who reads books written by liberals and then tries to preach them to the congregation. I would not give him a Lincoln penny, not even an old dull one. But if the fellow loves God, I am going to fellowship with him.

God will let a movement die and throw it on the fire if it does not keep close to the blood and close to the truth and close to God, and if a person does not keep Christ in it and keep right and keep morally sound and doctrinally sound. We keep a group alive by prayer and heart searching and good preaching and walking with God. So do not ever think for a minute that there are Christians inferior to you because they do not belong to your group.

Other Christians are dear to me. I am a catholic—you know what that means? That means a universal Christian. That means somebody that believes in the whole church of Christ, and I am that. I am not Roman Catholic, but I am a catholic. All of His children are my brothers and sisters; and they that love the Father love His children.

He that loves His Father loves His children. And he that loves the heavenly Father loves all of His children. I love them all. I love the little ladies with little black hats, and I love the men with beards, and I love the people who wear uniforms that look like the postman coming to deliver mail, and I love the Salvation Army and I love all the Lord's people, if they are the Lord's people. I will not go along with the liberals and the modernists and the God deniers or Christ deniers. I cannot go along with them, no matter if they call themselves Christians. So ask yourself, does this experience make you love all God's people? If it does, it is very likely of God. If it makes you feel superior to them or drives a wedge between you and them, chances are it is not of God.

Attitude Toward the World

What does this experience or this Scripture that we think we know the meaning of—this new interpretation—what does it do about *our attitude toward the world?* Does it excuse worldliness? Does it reason that because different people have different ideas of worldliness, we therefore cannot be sure? If it does, it is not of God. The truth will tend to separate us from the world and its ways and values. I think that it is a lamentable and grievous thing that the average rank and file of young women in America think that to be a movie star would be to reach the final pinnacle of all possible happiness and perfection. Why should they choose the lowest order of humanity and follow that as an example?

Why would they choose to have themselves photographed half-clad, day and night, before the camera, to feed the carnal, vicious lusts of men and women? And why should our lovely, sweet girls act so starry-eyed if they could just have their autograph, just touch them?

I was riding on a train one time when I saw an actress. I will not give her name, but she ate across from me, and somebody pointed her out and said that was so-and-so. She just looked like anybody else. I have sisters who look as good as she did. She just looked ordinary, just a little bitty woman. I then went back to my Pullman car after watching her eat. I opened the newspapers and my eyes fell upon this same woman advertising that there was a show coming to the town where we were going to put on one of her big deals. Boy, in the advertisement she looked as if she had had a permanent wave given her by the angel Gabriel and had borrowed her glamorous clothing from Gabriel. She looked as if she had dropped right out of heaven, the dust not off her wings yet. When I saw here in the dinner car she was just a homely, little woman sitting there looking like any other homely looking woman, but when they got through with her in the ad, she looked like somebody else.

Then we want our young people to imitate those phonies. If you want to imitate somebody, imitate Susanne Wesley. She had 17 kids, and John Wesley was the last one. You can thank God on your knees for the rest of your life that John Wesley was ever born. Thank God for Monica, the mother of Augustine, if you will. Thank God for good women. Pick missionaries and pastors' wives and saints in your church back home. Simple-hearted, glorious people with hearts that are wondrous and full of grace. Pick them and imitate them, and you will thank God all through eternity that you picked the right models. Do not pick the wrong model.

Any doctrine that makes the world your friend is not your friend. And any doctrine that makes it easy for you to hobnob with the world and the world's ways and accept the world's values, and do the way the world does, is not of God.

Attitude Toward Sin

Finally, what does that new interpretation of Scripture or that new experience or that new teaching affect *our attitude toward our relation to sin?* If it is of God, it will make sin intolerable.

The closer I come to God, the more intolerable sin becomes to me. Yet I have heard people who have had spiritual experiences say, "Sin is not sin to me anymore. God has made me holy inside. I cannot sin, and therefore, I can do these things that if other people did them they would be sin."

The devil certainly crawled up inside that fellow before he ever started teaching that doctrine. Sin is sin no matter who practices it. And if God will send a sinner to hell for sinning, how more ought His children never to practice sin. We ought to be saved from sin, brethren.

While I am not one who believes in what some would call Christian perfection, I believe there is such a thing as being cleansed from sin, walking in the Spirit and not fulfilling the lust of the flesh. And I believe that it is entirely within the right of any Christian to go to God and demand that God make him holy and keep him from sin. Of course, he may stumble. If he stumbles, there is a first-aid kit. "My little children, these things write I unto you, that ye sin not." That is the will of God, number one. "And if any man sin, we have an advocate with the Father" (1 John 2:1). That is the first-aid kit. The Lord does not let His stumbling children die. He picks them up, dusts them off, binds up their wounds and starts them all anew.

There is deliverance if we sin, but we should not be always making provision for sinning. If we make provision for sinning tomorrow, we will be sinning tomorrow. But if we go on our knees and say, "Lord, there's nothing good in me, but I believe that thou art my keeper, my sanctifier, and thou wilt keep me from sin," God will keep you from sin.

Those are the seven tests of whether an experience, a teaching, a miracle are of God. I exhort you to press on and test everything. If God has done something for you, thank Him with all of your heart and seek those things that are above where Christ sitteth on the right hand of God. The place up there is better than any can be down here. And there is nothing in this wide world that will be as wonderful as when we look upon His face and see Him as He is. If talking with Him here is wonderful, how much more wonderful will it be talking to Him without a veil.

A.W. TOZER:
THE AUTHORIZED
BIOGRAPHY

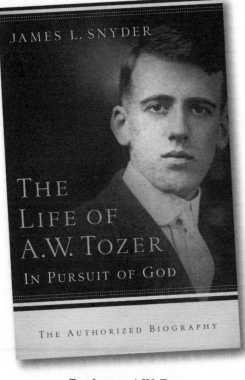

To understand the ministry of A.W. Tozer, it is important to know who he was, including his relationship with God. In *The Life of A.W. Tozer,* James L. Snyder lets us in on the life and times of a deep thinker who was not afraid to "tell it like it is" and never compromised his beliefs. A.W. Tozer's spiritual legacy continues today as his writings challenge readers to a deeper relationship and worship of God in reverence and adoration. Here is Tozer's life story, from boyhood to his conversion at the age of 17, to his years of pastoring and writing more than 40 books (at least two of which are regarded as Christian classics and continue to appear on bestseller lists today). Examining Tozer's life will allow you to learn from a prophet who had much to say against the compromises he observed in contemporary Christian living and the hope he found in his incredible God.

THE LIFE OF A.W. TOZER :
IN PURSUIT OF GOD
James L. Snyder
ISBN 978.08307.46941
ISBN 08307.46943

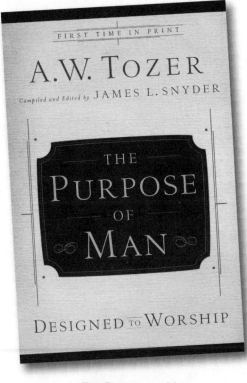